Jean-François Lyotard

Titles in the series Critical Lives present the work of leading cultural figures of the modern period. Each book explores the life of the artist, writer, philosopher or architect in question and relates it to their major works.

In the same series

Jean-François Lyotard

Kiff Bamford

REAKTION BOOKS

This book is dedicated to the memory of Frank Flynn

Published by Reaktion Books Ltd
Unit 32, Waterside
44–48 Wharf Road
London N1 7UX, UK

www.reaktionbooks.co.uk

First published 2017
Copyright © Kiff Bamford 2017

Printed and bound in Great Britain by Bell & Bain, Glasgow

A catalogue record for this book is available from the British Library

ISBN 978 1 78023 808 1

Contents

Lyotard, Villeneuve-lès-Avignon, summer 1985.

Introduction: Warning

In 1978 Jean-François Lyotard prepared a short television programme for the French channel FR3. In it, he refuses to conform to accepted conventions and plays with the usual format of presentation. Lyotard's voice is heard over a black screen: 'You are going to see him; you are going to hear him. You do not know who he is . . . '[1] When images do appear, they are, for the most part, out of sync with the soundtrack, as Lyotard embarks on a critique of his own discourse: why has he been brought before you? What are the criteria for assessing the role of a philosopher? 'I bet that he won't tell you anything about what he does' – he wagers – before finally declaring, 'This philosopher thus refuses to appear before your eyes and ears as an authority, as he is asked to do . . . '[2]

This book starts with a hesitancy, a mode of doubt. Perhaps the one constant throughout Lyotard's work is a distrust of unquestioned authority: hence any attempt to present the critical life of such a figure must proceed with caution. However, this fear of presenting something which might be considered a whole picture is assuaged to some extent by the absence of any written autobiography or biography on which to draw. This book will, therefore, have many holes and makes no claim to be either authoritative or comprehensive. Rather, it is hoped that this Critical Life will provide a number of routes into the dense undergrowth of his thought, which asks us to lose hold of what we think we already know.

As Lyotard doubted the assumptions made of his own authority as a philosopher in the television programme described above, I will similarly declare my own lack of authority in this introduction. I am neither French, nor a philosopher. Of course, it is more reassuring to read a book which adopts a confident tone and in which the narrative voice remains unquestioned. However, the hesitancy which I have already indicated is no mere ploy, but an integral part of the book itself: my position of quasi-ignorance leads to a heightened awareness of the need to explain the traditions, conventions and differences which accompany Lyotard's life and work. Similarly, an emphasis is deliberately placed on the significance of his thought beyond the traditional remit of philosophy. It is important, therefore, that this book is not written from the French context – in which Lyotard is clearly regarded as a philosopher – but from an anglophone experience, in which one is as likely to find Lyotard's work in sociology, cultural studies or politics, as in philosophy. I have previously written at length on the potential of Lyotard's thought for performance art, a topic about which he wrote very little, thereby demonstrating the potential of his provocations for future work, sometimes in unexpected fields.[3]

The diverse interests of Lyotard are echoed in the interdisciplinary approach of this book, exploring the relationship of his thought to politics, art, film and literature, in addition to the philosophical traditions and concerns of French thought. These multifaceted aspects of Lyotard's work are reflected in the complexity of his own life, which refuses to follow the clear trajectory common to academics in France, but rather stalls and detours, with fifteen years of political engagement being his first 'career'. To pretend that Lyotard's life can fit into the conventions of traditional biography would be to ignore the thrust of many of his philosophical arguments, which refute the premise of linear development along a sequence of points to a final destination. However, his struggle with thinking, his confrontation with the task of writing and thinking philosophy differently – and always politically – takes place within a series of very particular contexts and in response to people and places which play a significant role. Lyotard's engagements through politics, education and a continual dialogue with artists, writers and other thinkers makes his work shift and change. Resisting and responding to others with a warmth and enthusiasm of which his students, friends and family speak, the 'scintillating affectivity' Hugh J. Silverman describes combines with a challenge to respond.[4]

Lyotard's refusal to play the game expected of the philosopher invited to present himself on television – 'as usual on Mondays, here is our intellectual' – is one of many examples which makes those inclined to fall into the conventions of the biographical hesitate.[5] Why is there no biography of Lyotard (b. 1924)? It is an absence that singles him out from other figures in this series of Critical Lives, many of which draw on authorized biographies or are shortened versions by the same biographer – *Foucault* by David Macey, who was also the author of *The Lives of Michel Foucault*, is one such example. Lyotard's contemporaries are well served: in addition to Michel Foucault (b. 1926), there are several biographies of Jacques Derrida (b. 1930), and Lyotard's classmate and colleague, Gilles Deleuze (b. 1925), is similarly the subject of books with a biographical approach. Yet, of those philosophers and thinkers who constitute 'French thought' to those outside France, Lyotard is comparatively neglected. The term 'French thought' indicates the group of French philosophers, sociologists and psychoanalysts who became popular in anglophone academia – the United States, Canada, the United Kingdom and Australia in particular – during the later decades of the twentieth century. The term itself indicates a very particular reception of their work in academic disciplines, usually outside philosophy, and whose history of translation, publication and circulation has often resulted in a mutation of their initial ideas. The reception of French thought in America is well documented as a cultural phenomenon, and Lyotard's reception from the 1970s onwards, together with his role as a visiting professor outside France, will form an important part of this present story.

Although Lyotard is regarded as one of the major figures of French thought, his work is not widely known beyond the sometimes problematic association with that which is termed 'the postmodern'. Lyotard's name became so closely wedded to this single term, one which was also associated with a particular period of cultural production in the 1980s, that it became difficult to consider Lyotard outside this particular historical moment. Consequently, there remain many aspects of Lyotard's work which are overshadowed by the dominance of the postmodern, some of which are considered in this book, and biographical contexts remain little known. The aim of this book is to open up some of the lesser-known aspects of Lyotard's work through a discussion of his central ideas placed within the wider historical, political and cultural contexts of the second half of the twentieth century.

To read Lyotard is to be exposed to a relentless shift in style and form: it seems that each work demands a different use of language, not for the sake of novelty but so that the writing can be a conscious part of the thinking. When asked to contribute a foreword to *The Lyotard Reader*, a collection of translated texts published in 1989, Lyotard muses on the fact that the writer of a text is also its first reader: you therefore hear yourself writing. But this is too straightforward: what about when you listen to yourself writing? 'You end up listening to yourself writing when you have no faith in your style' – that is when the self-conscious intervention begins, the mode of doubt and uncertainty that makes 'you feel unworthy and anxious'.[6] It may result in an overwriting that annoys the reader, but such worries are good because they indicate that you are 'unsure of where you are, or completely lost', an undoing which is shown in the writing. As a consequence, it is often difficult to identify Lyotard's voice – there seems always to be an interlocutor, whether an imagined character in a dramatic dialogue or another philosopher, writer or artist, whose position Lyotard inhabits and then adapts to his own ends. In *The Differend*, for example, he plays with a quotation by the philosopher Vincent Descombes:

'You can't say everything' (Descombes, 1977). – Disappointed? Did you desire it? Or at least did something – 'language'– want it? Wanted to unfurl its full powers? A will? A life? A desire? a lack? These are so many teleologies of fulfilment, or melancholias for the unfulfilled.[7]

Confronted with this tone of ironic dismissal, this challenge to our intentions when embarking on any written project, any use of language – whether writing, hearing or listening – it becomes less surprising that the sometimes confrontational Lyotard has scared off those hunting a life story. Lyotard mocks our desire to say it all, to know it all, warning us against any neat tidying up and closing down of thought; his energy derives from an opening up to the mode of uncertainty which carries many different names: *Dérive*, 1968, *Les Immatériaux*, childhood. That is why this book is not a step towards an understanding of Lyotard's life and work, but an anxious passage through its fragmentation. It forces us to ask: in what ways can a life be traced without succumbing to a desire for fulfilment, or a melancholia 'for the unfulfilled'?

1

Openings

In 1996, two years before his death, but aware of the leukaemia which was to bring about his end, Lyotard published his last extensive work, *Signé Malraux* (Signed, Malraux). It was a biography. The choice of genre came as a surprise to some commentators, and it was set to confound expectations. Lyotard spoke of the choice of genre as another ruse, a way of approaching philosophy differently, 'risking philosophical thought in a genre which is foreign, seen as hostile to it', and in so doing following the alternative autobiography of André Malraux, his *Anti-Memoirs*.[1] Coincidentally, shortly after the release of Lyotard's book, Malraux was admitted to the pantheon of French gods, quite literally: on the twentieth anniversary of Malraux's death, his ashes were ceremoniously transferred to the Panthéon, the national mausoleum which dominates the Latin Quarter of the Parisian Left Bank. While somewhat unsettled by the ceremony of secular deification and the inevitable adoption by the state, Lyotard felt that this event was an appropriate contribution to the myth Malraux had created from his life:

> in this melancholic gesture we all feel a plucking at the
> heart: the poetic and historic epic of which Malraux is
> one of the eminent figures, will we ever see it again?[2]

The writer, resistance fighter, aesthetician and – for a decade – Minister of Culture as part of General de Gaulle's government was

André Malraux at home, with images from *Le Musée imaginaire*, vol. II, in 1953.

a paradoxical figure. The complexities of Malraux are pasted together by Lyotard into a narrative, but one that trips and jumps, fixating on the abject elements in both life and fiction: the uncertainty between *bios* and *graphia*. Lyotard's approach in *Signed, Malraux* echoes the non-linear, anachronic juxtapositions that famously populate Malraux's museum of the mind, his *musée imaginaire*, which Lyotard describes as follows:

> André had often visited the Musée Guimet and his eye
> was already attuned to Buddhist sculptures and Persian
> miniatures. But now he saw what he would do in *The Voices*

of Silence: he could place the Reims angel and a fourth-century Gandhara head side by side, on facing pages. Not, of course, to extract some essence of a man-who-smiles or to imagine some influence leading from one work to the other, but to show an insistent kinship between all forms – one that is nonthematic: 'They impose the presence of another world. Not necessarily an infernal or paradisiac one and not only an afterworld, but *a present beyond* '.[3]

Despite clear differences between Lyotard and Malraux – in their politics and written style, for example – it is difficult to read *Signed, Malraux* without hearing Lyotard's thinking behind the voice of its subject. To describe his venture into biography, Lyotard coined the term 'hypobiography', modestly hiding this in the acknowledgements at the back of the French edition but subsequently highlighted by many commentators, including his colleague Philippe Bonnefis. Is this a hypothetical biography, muses Bonnefis: 'what remains of narration in a life story when the event is uncertain'?[4]

Uncertainty, hesitation – images cut together to form a sweeping impression of remembered fragments. Lyotard had once hoped his Malraux might become a cinematic event. When Bonnefis informs us of this, the quickly drawn vignettes of life seen by the toddler Malraux, which populate the opening scene of *Signed, Malraux,* rise up to the scale of the big screen:

> And, from the hearse heading down by way of Place Clichy, the little guy could look out with his big peepers and see a hackney coach going by, a bearded man in a derby, an omnibus, bare-headed errand girls with their basket on their arm, a white percheron hauling milk cans, ditch-diggers with their trousers held up by Zouave's sashes, steaming piles of horse manure, a cabriolet automobile, quarry stone facades decorated with nymphs, haberdashery signs and those of café concerts.[5]

The opening of Lyotard's own life, however, lacked a similar drama – or would need a cache of similarly cinematic devices to make it rise to something close to epic. There were, however, big, blue summer skies which he recalled in a short late text, 'Foreword: Spaceship', one of many occasional pieces he wrote out of friendship, or a sense of obligation, and which often demonstrate the ease with which stories can simultaneously both suggest a freedom of imagination and pose a question:

> Years ago my sister and I would go off with two or three little friends, on long bicycle rides into the blue Atlantic summer, with our parents' blessing and our day's supplies of food on our carriers. Perhaps going to school has only ever been to fill in time between radiant holidays . . .[6]

This same blue sky of the Vendée plays a critical role in the discussion of presence in painting in the opening section of *Que peindre?* (What to Paint?), his gathering of aesthetic meditations published in 1987. The blue is an inexact memory, a feeling which escapes attempts to render it to language, an event. 'Such is presence; the sensory event, if you will' offers the character 'HE' in this dialogue between two positions, here circling round the need to represent such a sky – the blue, the feeling – but arguing instead for a recognition of its importance in awakening that which has been forgotten.[7] The role of the forgotten, or more particularly that which has not been forgotten but which cannot be recalled, plays an important role in Lyotard's later writings. But wait! A childhood vignette used to recall a sensation which cannot be forgotten, by a writer who is seemingly against nostalgia and melancholia? A word of warning is necessary.

In Lyotard's writings seemingly paradoxical positions often appear; they act to lure us in and trip us up, in order to confound our expectations. It is important to highlight such a case here.

The terms 'childhood' and 'infant' are not used by Lyotard to idealize the developmental period we call childhood: the 'infant' is, rather, a mode of thinking which has no correlation to the age of the thinker. 'Maybe there is more childhood available to thought at thirty-five than at eighteen, and more outside a degree course than in one.'[8] This call to interrupt our linear understanding of time is an important and recurrent theme of Lyotard's work. Already we have noted the temporal juxtapositions in Malraux's *Musée imaginaire*, not brought together for humour but because of what it does: the presence it brings and the childhood of thought, which does not correlate to a particular age. However, there is a risk to this adaptation of existing terms: 'childhood', which is not childhood, and – the misunderstanding which will dog his later years – 'the postmodern'. The common assumption that the prefix 'post' would mean 'after' in a chronological sense has been the source of much misunderstanding, and clouds the importance of Lyotard's rejection of time as a linear construct:

> A work can become modern only if it is first postmodern. Thus understood, postmodernism is not modernism at its end, but in a nascent state, and this state is recurrent.[9]

The life of Jean-François Lyotard is a life of non sequiturs and ironic juxtapositions: born near the seat of French royalty in Versailles, a leftist radical who wrote of the repression of the French military in Algeria while being paid to teach the children of officers in a military academy, it is as well that Lyotard had no belief in destiny. Unlike Malraux, who would edit out those aspects of his life which did not fit the myth he created, Lyotard fought against the elements which jarred and rubbed. Jean-François Lyotard was born on 10 August 1924, not into the literary bourgeoisie, but part of the aspirational middle class: his father, Jean-Pierre Lyotard, was a sales representative for a cloth manufacturer, selling to private individuals, companies and shops throughout France. Jean-Pierre came from a background of absolute poverty: his parents were peasants from the rural centre of France, yet he knew both Latin and ancient Greek, which he taught to his children and grandchildren.[10] Having been singled out by a schoolteacher because of his talent and interest in school, Jean-Pierre was looked after by the Jesuits, attending a small seminary – hence the Classical education. He survived the First World War, having been exposed to gas attacks and receiving a leg injury, which meant he subsequently walked with a slight limp. As most veterans of the war of 1914–18 did, he retained a very clear sense of its horror, and it remained, for him, the decisive factor influencing subsequent events in the twentieth century. Uncommonly for this period, Lyotard's father lived until the age of 89: he died in November 1965, just before Jean-François Lyotard left the political group Pouvoir Ouvrier (P. O.), which had broken from Socialisme ou Barbarie (S. ou B.) two years earlier.

According to Lyotard's daughters, Jean-François had a great admiration for his father, one which extended beyond the general respect given to ex-servicemen after the war. It was clear that Jean-Pierre saw in his son the academic and intellectual possibilities he had not had the opportunity to realize for himself. A man of great self-discipline, Jean-Pierre would regularly follow a routine while on holiday in the Vendée: descending to the beach in his dressing gown, he would swim across the bay and back, get out and return to the house, regardless of the weather and time of year.[11] While Lyotard's father's ambition for the young Lyotard was to pursue the intellectual course which had been closed to him, his mother invested in Jean-François all her hopes for the family – he was regarded by her as the son and heir, which made their subsequent break particularly difficult. In a posthumous tribute to Lyotard, the philosopher Alain Badiou, a Marxist and Maoist agitator during many of their shared years at the University of Paris VIII, spoke of the many breaks that

Lyotard had to endure – the political breaks before, during and after Lyotard's membership of Socialisme ou Barbarie and the names he gave to these in his writings: 'the intractable' and 'the differend'.[12] What Badiou does not mention is that these breaks began with his family: again, an intractable difference of politics.

When Jean-Pierre married Lyotard's mother, Madeleine Cavalli, she was already a war widow. Her first husband had been killed early in the war, while she was pregnant with Henriette, Lyotard's half-sister. Lyotard's closest sibling was his sister Josette; three years his elder, it was she with whom he took the holiday bicycle rides under the blue Vendée sky.

In a late interview given in the context of the Malraux biography, Lyotard laughs off the interviewer's attempts to develop a biographical line of enquiry – 'Ah, you want me to fall into biographical idiocy. At my age . . .'[13] Just as he rejected the simplistic psycho-biographic readings of art by Sigmund Freud, Lyotard follows Malraux's horror at the idea that events in the life of an artist or writer could 'explain' his work. Indeed, Lyotard's desire to wander is always away from the assignation of meaning: the resistance to representation in the discussion of the presence of blue, prompted by the sky, is because such representation kills that which maintains its pertinence as 'presence'. And yet there is something in the movements that occur within the family of the young Lyotard which sets a course for a battle of far-reaching consequences.

We perhaps gain an insight into the conservative nature of the family through the knowledge that his half-sister married the son of a member of the upper classes and that his sister Josette married young into a family with a noble title. Although Josette had been taught Latin and Greek by her father, it was the intellectual aspirations of Jean-François that were encouraged; Josette was married before her educational potential was realized, breaking off her medical studies.

The concerns of Lyotard's mother – for aristocratic circles and the strong family ties associated with the tradition of French Catholicism – lead one to think that she was part of the silent majority in France who did not oppose the arrival of Marshal Pétain. This is the political situation from which Lyotard pushed himself: 'politically I knew nothing', he said of his early years – he was aged just fifteen at the outbreak of the Second World War and still fifteen at the armistice, signed nine months later.[14] The speed with which France was overcome by the military strength of Hitler's German forces is most often attributed to a combination of outdated military tactics and hardware and a determination to avoid a repetition of the still-recent devastation of the war of 1914–18. The negotiations which led to a tripartite division of France were initially seen by many as a pragmatic move, allowing a large part of the country – broadly the South, but excluding Bordeaux and the western coastline – to retain an autonomous government under the name 'Free France'. When the 84-year-old Marshal Pétain put himself forward as leader of Free France, his status as a hero of the war of 1914–18 convinced many that he was, indeed, a national hero responding to the patriotic call of his country in a time of crisis. This was a view held in particular by the religious right and those attracted to his call for an authoritarian redress of the loucheness he identified in the pre-war Third Republic: he was considered a necessary moderating force who would, for example, protect the Jewish minority. He did not. Support for Pétain extended to the occupied zone – covering the North and West of France, including its coastline and retaining Paris as its administrative capital – where little comparative autonomy existed.

Perhaps more important is the extent to which such support continued as Pétain's position became increasingly compromised: the compulsory civilian service; the declaration in 1942 that he hoped for a German victory; the conscription of French labourers to work in Germany and an official anti-Semitism that included French assistance in the deportation of a large proportion of the country's Jewish population, a quarter of whom were exterminated. As Lyotard himself wrote in 1948, reflecting on the inheritance of his generation:

> We come out of the twentieth century's most concrete achievement, the war, in a state of monstrous poverty. We were twenty when the camps vomited into our laps those whom there had not been time or energy to digest.[15]

Politically, Lyotard was yet to have the awakening he credits completely to his experiences in Algeria in 1950–52, but in the years immediately after the war, a series of realizations occurred that shifted his own position dramatically.

Lyotard's upbringing was Catholic. We have already mentioned the debt his father's learning owed to the Jesuits, but his education was, as he wrote, *à la française* – that is, not the doxa of Italian Catholicism and tempered by the laicity of the French state.[16] Nevertheless, Lyotard was a church chorister, and in his youth he had considered the priesthood, or more specifically taking orders as a Dominican monk. This often-quoted anecdote comes from his contribution to the annual Wellek lecture series, held at the University of California, Irvine: three lectures delivered in 1986 in response to a request 'to define "my position" in the field of criticism and the path which led me to this position'.[17] In order to do this, Lyotard opened the lecture series by describing his uncertain desires as a child of eleven or twelve, wavering between different vocations: a Dominican monk, a painter or a historian. These three childish wishes are then used to outline three preoccupations within his work: law, colour and form, and event, which give the subtitle to the subsequent publication, *Peregrinations: Law, Form, Event*, something close to an intellectual biography. We must, therefore, be cautious when repeating these

Lyotard at the Lycée Buffon, Paris. Second row down, fourth from the right, aged about 11 years old.

childhood aspirations simply as biography, as often happens, but their wavering – their feeling of hesitancy – highlights the breadth of Lyotard's own interests. This breadth is significant for his work as someone who 'does philosophy', not only as a philosopher but as someone who is unable to take a fixed 'position': drifting across demarcations, led by 'the lightness of thoughts . . . Thoughts are clouds . . . pushed and pulled at variable speeds.'[18]

In the 1930s Lyotard's family had moved from Versailles to the centre of Paris, near Montparnasse, living at 59 Boulevard de Vaugirard, which was close to the Lycée Buffon, where Lyotard was a pupil from 1935 to 1942. The vignette of childhood that opens *Peregrinations* also reveals Lyotard's early interest in literature: writing poems, short stories and essays from the age of fourteen or fifteen and then, aged twenty, a novel. His literary ambitions, like those of the painter and historian, would eventually be re-routed through philosophy, and the 'sacrificial' aspect of his monastic desires transformed into the years spent with Socialisme ou Barbarie and Pouvoir Ouvrier (1954–66), engaged in 'political reflection and praxis'.[19]

The Second World War had shaken Lyotard's attitude to life, an attitude he describes as having been 'poetic, introspective and solitary', reflecting his study of the philosophy and psychology of indifference.[20] One of the few references to his time at the Lycée Buffon is an embarrassed illustration of his own naivety. When Jewish schoolmates arrived at the Lycée wearing yellow stars – a requirement in Paris by June 1942 – he and a friend turned up the following day with stars sewn onto their own clothes in solidarity: 'as a provocation. It was completely thoughtless. Idiotic.'[21] This was not an isolated event in Paris, as several memoirs of the occupation recall, but they were most often acts of youthful rebellion, rather than considered, political acts.[22] What Lyotard only became fully aware of later was the extent of an active resistance network at his school, which was made public through the arrest of its leader, professor Raymond Burgard, by the Gestapo in April 1942. This provoked public protests by student members, who continued with their acts of defiance and sabotage, leading to the arrest and imprisonment of five students of the Lycée Buffon, who were condemned to death in October 1942. The five pupils were shot at the stand de tir de Balard on 8 February 1943 and are now honoured as 'The Five Martyrs of the Lycée Buffon'.

It is not clear what awareness Lyotard had of the activities of the resistance while at Buffon, having completed his baccalaureate in June 1942; he only later discovered some of his friends' involvement. The sense of guilt that this may have induced in him would perhaps burn slowly: given his parents' politics, it is clear that friends would know to be careful with sensitive information. However, in contrast to the acts of rebellion and defiance by the few, it is useful to read an essay by a classmate and friend of Lyotard, Pierre Gripari, who later became an author and well-known children's writer. Gripari was one of three young men, including Lyotard and Paul Viallaneix, asked by the journal *Les Temps modernes* to write an account of their generation's experience. Collected under the title 'Born in 1925', Gripari's contribution focused on reconciliation, through an emphasis on the different, widespread forms of collaboration. It acts as a useful redress to the myth of resistance which became an integral part of post-war French history.

> In 1940, like all good French we were 'all behind the Marshal'. Some completely, whilst others found a way to be Gaullist at the same time. Only later, came the differentiation of blame between this one and the other. My family was Gaullist. But everywhere: at school, in the city, we rubbed shoulders with very intelligent people who did not hide being pro-German, and who said, well, things not so absurd, and in French as pure as ours.[23]

Lyotard's contribution to *Les Temps modernes* – founded by Jean-Paul Sartre, Simone de Beauvoir and Maurice Merleau-Ponty in October 1945 – was less personal than Gripari's, but similarly refused to make nationalistic assertions. Lyotard extended the editor's viewpoint – the perspective of three young French men – to acknowledge the experiences of those in other European situations: 'we were fifteen in 1940. For a Czech, that means clandestine action; for a German, *Gott mit uns*; for a French person, introversion.'[24] But Lyotard is still clear that it is the experience of a particular youth that he gives, an intellectual youth, and questions the collective 'we' he is asked to represent, anticipating a question central to *The Differend*, more than three decades later. There is a tone to Lyotard's essay which suggests that he is part of a generation grown old before its time, but, unlike other post-war periods, there has been no overthrow of old ideals: 'we have not laid waste what our predecessors held dear; those attachments have simply died out.'[25] Gripari refers to 'the class of '45' – an ironic nomenclature that is never used – as one that has been forgotten, missed out: called neither to the compulsory work service (STO) of the Vichy regime nor for military service. Lyotard's direct experience of fighting came in the summer of 1944 while a first aider during the liberation of Paris, a time he alludes to much later when teaching a seminar in Germany in the years immediately prior to German reunification. His discourse reflects on the role of the German language and culture in his upbringing: poetic, philosophical – 'Throughout my life, Germans on my bedside table', but also 'the moan of a young dying soldier, "Mutter", on a stretcher in the aid station at the Passage Saint André des Arts, July 1944, Paris.'[26]

The importance of German thought for French culture, and philosophy in particular, was again made clear to Lyotard in the years after the Lycée Buffon, when he attended one of the most prestigious *lycées* in Paris, Louis-le-Grand. The peculiarities of the French higher education system need some explanation here, in order to understand why, having taken his baccalaureate, Lyotard did not move straight to university. The elite institutions of the higher education system in France are not the universities but the *grandes écoles*. This grouping of institutions was founded after the revolution to educate the leaders of the French Republic – judges, administrators, scientists, but also philosophers and writers. The *grandes écoles* do not have award-giving powers and therefore their students are also enrolled in a university, but they are predominantly independent with their own traditions, student slang and highly regarded professors. The *grande école* to which a *lycée* would wish its philosophy students to aspire to gain entry was, and still remains, the École Normale Supérieure (ENS), whose roll call of past pupils includes Henri Bergson, Jean-Paul Sartre and Michel Foucault. In order to prepare to take the intensely competitive entrance exam, students enrol on a two-year programme of preparatory classes, named *hypokhâgne* and *khâgne*. These classes, CPGE (*classes préparatoires aux grandes écoles*), are taught at many *lycées*; Lyotard could have stayed at the Lycée Buffon, for example, but the Lycée Louis-le-Grand, which sits next to the Sorbonne on rue Saint-Jacques, had a greater success rate. It was at Louis-le-Grand that Lyotard studied the three German thinkers referred to as the 'three Hs', Hegel, Husserl and Heidegger, taking particular inspiration from the philosopher Ferdinand Alquié, who taught him in *hypokhâgne*.

However, Lyotard failed the entrance exam to the ENS and instead continued his studies at the Sorbonne; he had perhaps written in too literary a style for the examiners, he later reflected. It was the fact that Lyotard did not attend the ENS that set him apart from many of his contemporaries, more than the failure itself, which was not unusual: Sartre and Foucault failed the first time, while Derrida took three times to pass. The division and consequent elitism of those who attended the ENS, the *normaliens*, has been commented upon widely and analysed in depth by Pierre Bourdieu, as part of his broader analysis of the hierarchies and self-perpetuating structures of power in the French education system. Part of Bourdieu's analysis also concerns the next examination-based hurdle to academic life in France: the *agrégation*, which was needed at the time in order to gain a teaching position at a *lycée* or university. This experience was again a difficult one for Lyotard, who achieved admissibility to the oral examination, via a series of demanding written papers, in both 1948 and 1949, but did not pass the oral examination until 1950. This final success was remarkable because it came at a time of great personal adversity and distraction. In 1950 Lyotard was already married with a young child and engaged in his first teaching position, away from Paris. Yet he was placed fourth in the *agrégation* of 1950, from a field of several hundred, a year when only sixteen male students (and seven female, ranked separately) were admitted to the ranks of those qualified to teach philosophy classes, compulsory in the final year of the baccalaureate.[27] The personal tumult of these few years is difficult to comprehend: there was a significant break with his family – a rupture which came from increasing political differences,

Jean-François and Andrée Lyotard, Les Sables d'Olonne, *c.* 1950.

in some ways made manifest in the figure of Andrée May, whom Lyotard had married in 1948. Andrée May was not the wife Lyotard's mother had hoped her only son would marry; although she was bright, she had no title, no fortune, came from a Jewish family and, by the time of their marriage, was pregnant with their first child.

2

Politics

The personal tumult of these few years is difficult to comprehend. I confessed in the last chapter: I have been circling around the personal aspects of Lyotard's life story and suggesting the problematic nature of biography for Lyotard himself. I have felt a particular unease at describing the personal attributes and feelings of his family: terse statements about political positions hide a complex web of contradictions and emotional attachments. Then I came upon an interview, published in the u.s. journal *Diacritics* in 1984, which Lyotard gave to Georges Van Den Abbeele, the translator of *Le Différend* (The Differend). Attached to the interview is a short piece by Lyotard titled 'Decor'. It is a minor piece, not dissimilar to 'Spaceship', the text which gave us the blue sky of the last chapter – the result of a request by a translator or an editor for a little something to add to his own work, to make a publication more appealing, such was Lyotard's attraction in the 1980s – but its content is far from minor, and neither is Lyotard's rationale for its inclusion.

In little more than seven hundred words, with no pause for paragraphs, Lyotard fires out snippets of scenes from the crises which have made up the 'context of my work' – the war, liberation, the war in Algeria, the events of 1968 – slammed together. Lyotard explains that the purpose of these vignettes – queuing for food, shots in the street, Algerians frisked – is to highlight the difference between the specific context of his work and that of the Anglo-American public, a difference he terms *le différend* (the differend). The complexity of this term needs some unpacking, and the wider implications of Lyotard's usage will be developed throughout the book, but I begin here with a simple description of the term. The differend indicates a situation in which two parties are unable to reconcile their differences, not because of a recognized complaint, but because they lack a means of communication, necessary for judgement, which doesn't privilege one party over another. A frequently quoted summary by Lyotard comes from section twelve of *The Differend*: 'I would like to call a *differend* the case where the plaintiff is divested of the means to argue and becomes for that reason a victim.'[1] The snapshots given in 'Decor' highlight sites of conflict – in Algeria, in the street, in the family – some of which are analysed further in *The Differend*. What strikes me here, in the close proximity of events, is the sense of a recurrent *feeling* of the differend, an aspect which becomes central to Lyotard's later writings on affect, on childhood and on the return of that which cannot be forgotten: anamnesis.

> My father comes home, throws his thick briefcase stuffed with coupons and fabric samples on the table, and says to my mother: Fischbacher is closing shop, I no longer have my representative's card. We wait in line at the soup kitchen at the other end of the Boulevard de Vaugirard. In the railway station of Sables d'Olonne, we distribute help and soup to old people evacuated from the Ardennes. The smell of piss, ether and bad coffee. At the exit to the community centre in Constantine, the CRS [Special Police Force] frisk our Algerian comrades, up against the wall with their hands in the air. They do not frisk me. She and I have decided to keep the child, I am out of work, my family does not like Jews, or secretaries, or unwed mothers.[2]

It is this last sentence which helps to reinforce the tumult of the situation I began to describe at the end of the last chapter:

'She and I have decided to keep the child, I am out of work, my family does not like Jews, or secretaries, or unwed mothers.' The implications of this collision of factors, sandwiched between the politics of the liberation, the increased talk of the resistance – of which Lyotard was not a part – and then his posting to Algeria in 1950, foreshadow the most important concern of his life and work: politics. Whether militant engagement or philosophical provocation, there is a connection back to the crucible of these tumultuous years as a young man in his mid-twenties.

In 1947 Lyotard had met Andrée May in Les Sables d'Olonne, in the Vendée; she would be his wife for more than fifty years. She taught him English, when his international career made it a necessity, and heightened his awareness of the 'Jewish question', at a time when silence was often the most common, and most telling, response to what had happened in Europe. Andrée May's father was an Alsatian Jew from an assimilated family, who became marked by his Jewish identity because of the war: he was deported, and returned ruined and weakened, dying soon after his return. Although Andrée's mother – Marguerite May (née Potier) – was not Jewish by birth, the circumstances of her own marriage, and the anti-Semitism in France at the time, meant that she had broken with her own family and was, therefore, completely integrated into her husband's Jewish family. Consequently, while Andrée May was only half-Jewish, she was very aware of her Jewish identity, culturally and psychologically, a fact forced on her during the war: her family were dispersed or exterminated; one of her uncles, Charles May, died in Auschwitz. As implied by Lyotard in the last section of the extract cited above, and reiterated by their daughters, Andrée entered Lyotard's family marked by many stains (*taches*): she had been unable to finish her studies because of her father's deportation and the need for her and her mother to hide themselves; afterwards, she had to go straight out to work.[3]

Jean-François and Andrée Lyotard, Les Sables d'Olonne, *c*. 1952.

The closeness of Andrée to her own mother – through the period of her father's internment, deportation and illness – was to continue throughout their lives. This close female bond is touchingly recounted in the one book she published in her own name, *L'Espace Marguerite: Empreintes d'enfance* (Marguerite Space: Imprints of Childhood, 1999). Later, having returned to finish her studies, she taught linguistics at university and translated several academic texts, but it was following her divorce from Lyotard in 1991, and her mother's death in 1993, that she responded to the call to write for herself, a 'fiction from reminiscences'.[4] Published after Lyotard's death, it places him in the background, the figure behind the camera taking the photograph of his wife and her mother, with whom he shared a large part of his life. Andrée describes the ease with which their new family took shape: after her father's death, she asked her mother to live with them; this meant that it was Lyotard and the children who were the 'newcomers', fitting into an already established pattern of life.[5] The decision came while Lyotard was studying for his second attempt at the *agrégation* oral examination, and he agreed without hesitation. Having been 'strangled by the oral', and his own timidity at the first attempt, he did not take up a teaching post in 1948, but was financially obliged to do so the following year.[6]

For the academic year 1949–50, Lyotard was posted away from Paris to teach in a military college in Burgundy: L'École militaire préparatoire d'Autun, referred to historically as a school for the *enfants de troupe*, the sons or orphans of soldiers below officer rank. Having finally succeeded in the oral and achieved the status of *agrégé* in 1950, Lyotard was posted to teach philosophy in *terminale*, the last year of the baccalaureate, in Algeria. The Lycée d'Aumale, Constantine, was in the then capital of the French *département* of Constantine in East Algeria. Although Lyotard only taught in Algeria for two years, it was to have a profound effect on him. After his return to mainland France, he followed the events of the

Front de Libération Nationale (FLN) and the war for independence
(1954–62) with critical commentary and practical involvement.

> When the group Socialism or Barbarism gave me responsibility
> for the Algerian section in 1955, Algeria did not name a
> 'question' of revolutionary politics for me, it was also the
> name of a debt. I owed and I owe my awakening, *tout court*,
> to Constantine. The differend showed itself with such a
> sharpness that the consolations then common among my
> peers (vague reformism, pious Stalinism, futile leftism)
> were denied to me. This humiliated people, once risen up,
> would not compromise. But at the same time, they did
> not have the means of achieving what is called liberty.[7]

This was written by Lyotard in 1989, under the title 'The Name
of Algeria', as an introduction to the publication *La Guerre
des Algériens* (The War of the Algerians). This collection of his
political writings on Algeria, which had first appeared in the
eponymous journal of the militant Marxist group Socialisme ou
Barbarie (S. ou B.) between 1956 and 1963, was published at the
request of Mohammed Ramdani. Identified simply as 'still an
Algerian student', Ramdani edited and introduced the collection,
opening his own introduction with the complaint that 35 years
after the start of the Algerian War, on 1 November 1954, the topic
'remains a taboo subject'.[8] Lyotard's analysis of the situation is
important, suggests Ramdani, because of his recognition of the
differends which exist within the situation, one that was echoed
by the turbulent history of the group S. ou B. which discussed
the events, and Lyotard's presentation of them, as its principal
correspondent on the Algerian situation. As is clear from the use
of the term 'differend' by both Lyotard and Ramdani in 1989,
this is a reconsideration of earlier writings through recourse to
later concepts, but this is also its strength. It is not simply an

SOCIALISME

OU BARBARIE

Organe de Critique et d'Orientation Révolutionnaire

PARAIT TRIMESTRIELLEMENT

Cover of the journal *Socialisme ou Barbarie*, vol. IV/21 (1957), featuring Lyotard's article 'A New Phase in the Algerian Question', written under the pseudonym F. Laborde.

analysis after the fact, but a reciprocal reflective process which highlights the importance of this period of Lyotard's writings, and identifies why it should not be separated from those which are better known. The absence of an English translation of Ramdani's essay is regrettable, as it gives an important foil to Lyotard's own introduction, which is available in English together with most of the *S. ou B.* essays in the collection *Political Writings* of 1993.

When Lyotard speaks of his debt to Algeria, it is not to suggest that he has been able to write from a position of understanding the situation: it was clear to Lyotard that this was the Algerians' war, a struggle of a very specific and particular nature. What Lyotard had encountered in Algeria, however, was a colonialism which shocked him. Although constitutionally the most populated areas of northern Algeria had been a part of France since 1848, the cultural, linguistic and economic division between European settlers (known as 'pieds noirs') and the indigenous, largely Muslim, population was marked. French institutions, including the education system, were dominated by the pied noir population and officials posted from mainland France, of which Lyotard was himself an example. The three *départements* of Constantine, Oran and Alger had officially been a part of metropolitan France for more than a century and consequently French culture dominated the lives of the pied noir population, which numbered approximately one million, while for the eight million members of Berber-Arab-Muslim population, there were varying degrees of integration. In 1954 school attendance for the *colon* population (the population with European ancestry) was five times that of the indigenous population, according to official statistics, while Lyotard relates that in 1950 the disparity was even greater.[9] The difficulty of finding an adequate terminology to write about these different communities – all of whom were officially French subjects, but not all citizens – highlights one of the paradoxes which shadows contemporary discussion of the unfurling events during the period of the war, a war which France did not recognize as such but simply as internal problems, or 'events'.[10] When Jacques Soustelle, governor-general of Algeria, declared, 'we must not, at any price, in any way and under any pretext, lose Algeria', the collective 'we', and the insistence on its unity in the face of evidence to the contrary, led to the terror of totalization.[11] The result, in Algeria, has been estimated at up to one million dead and a similar number displaced.[12]

Against the odds, the collective 'we' is employed to assert a collective belonging: 'we, the French people' is asserted through a process of self-authorization, normalizing an implicit obligation on the part of those being addressed and those who give voice to the assertion, a normative phrase. Therefore the assertion – 'we must not lose Algeria' – adopts the shared obligation which is inherent in the first person plural 'we' without authorization, leaving a rhetoric of performance which seeks to enact without authority. Or perhaps it is sufficient, asks Lyotard, for such a phrase to be formulated as a normative phrase and thereby obligate the addressee despite its lack of legitimation: the performative in this case is no mere rhetoric of performance but obligates, without recourse to a legitimating phrase.[13] Soustelle did not remain in post long enough to witness the granting of special powers to French authorities in Algeria, in 1956. These powers effectively distanced French representatives from French law, as exemplified by the officially sanctioned hijacking of an Air Maroc plane carrying five FLN leaders by the French military, in October 1956. As Lyotard wrote, in 1958, of the contradictions in both France and Algeria,

there is already no longer an *Algérie française*, in that 'France' is no longer present in any form in Algeria: in the countryside, there is an FLN administration; in the cities, there is an extremist administration. Paris is present nowhere . . . But France is saturated by Algeria through every pore.[14]

Lyotard's posting to Constantine in October 1950 was not unusual; François Châtelet, his classmate from the Sorbonne, had been named to Oran two years earlier, and the historian Pierre Souyri was teaching not far from Constantine, in Philippeville (now Skikda). However, the flow of young scholars between Algeria and mainland France was not one way – at least for the European (pied noir) population, Albert Camus being the most famous cultural émigré. Educated at the University of Algeria, Camus was forced to leave Algeria for Paris in 1940 following the closure of the left-wing newspaper for which he wrote by the Vichy-controlled authorities. Following his involvement in the resistance newspaper *Combat* and the publication of novels – including *L'Étranger* (The Outsider, 1942) and *La Peste* (The Plague, 1947) – he became embraced as a symbol of French culture, especially that of resistance.

Other culturally significant figures born in Algeria at this time, at least in terms of French literature and philosophy, include Jacques Derrida and Hélène Cixous; both from Sephardic Jewish families, they experienced upbringings which were different from those of other pied noir families, experiences intimated in the title of a short piece by Cixous: *Pieds-nus* (Bare Feet).[15] *Pieds-nus* divests the term 'pied noir' of its commonly held origin, as referring to the shiny black leather shoes of the early colonialists, in contrast to the unshod feet of the indigenous population. The term *Pieds-nus* questions the assumption that there was simply a division between Algerians of European origin and indigenous Algerians, one that ignores both the complexities of Berber and Arab communities and the racial hierarchies within the collective nomenclature 'pieds noirs' – an assumption which was questioned when the right to French citizenship was withdrawn for Jewish families living in Algeria in 1940. A quota system for Jewish children in Algerian schools, implemented in 1941 and extended in 1942, meant that the young Derrida was turned away from his *lycée* and reallocated to an improvised Jewish school, set up by Jewish teachers forced out of their positions – an expulsion which resulted in an equally forced integration for Derrida.[16]

Younger than Lyotard, Derrida had already left Algeria by the time of Lyotard's arrival; having completed the first year of the CPGE – the *hypokhâgne* – at the Lycée Bugeaud in Algiers, he left for Paris in 1949 to complete *khâgne* as a boarder at the Lycée Louis-le-Grand; no *lycée* in Algeria offered the *khâgne* preparatory class. Six years later, Cixous also attended the Lycée Bugeaud, which, unlike Louis-le-Grand, was co-educational, and completed her studies in English at the University of Bordeaux; much later she would play a key role in developing the experimental university at Vincennes, which was to become the University of Paris VIII – Lyotard's academic home for sixteen years (1971–87).

In *Peregrinations*, Lyotard explains that on leaving university, he felt the need to compensate for the omissions of his philosophical education: he read Marx, became involved in union activities and made contact with the Algerian liberation movements. It was at a union meeting late in 1950 that Lyotard first encountered Pierre Souyri (1925–1979), who was to be his political guide and fellow traveller for the next sixteen years; they joined S. ou B. together in 1954 and led the splinter group Pouvoir Ouvrier (Workers' Power), until Lyotard's departure in 1966. It is clear from Lyotard's homage to Souyri, 'Memorial to Marxism', that Lyotard's sense of debt to Souyri was huge: speaking of their first three years of comradeship, he wrote, 'he taught me everything except what the Algerians themselves taught me.'[17] Although they were of a similar age, Souyri's previous political experience was significantly different, his Marxist critique being based on encounters with, and a practical involvement in, several different groups and positions: at the age of seventeen, he joined the clandestine Communist Party of Aveyron and also held responsibilities in the rural resistance. In August 1944 he resigned from the Communist Party, made contact with Trotskyists and in 1946 joined the Fourth International, but by 1949 Souyri had abandoned Trotskyism and was posted to Philippeville, close to Constantine. The result of these experiences, according to Lyotard, was that Souyri already knew 'from experience and reflection what constitutes a class point of view' and had the resolve to maintain this. 'In short, he intimidated me.'[18]

'Memorial for Marxism' was written by Lyotard as a preface to Souyri's book *Révolution et contre-révolution en Chine.* Published in 1982, after Souyri's death, it also appeared in the journal *Esprit*, and was included in *Peregrinations* as an example of the differend that this later Lyotard found with Marxism, and consequently with his friend Souyri. The essay simultaneously develops an account of Souyri's approach and that of the group S. ou B.; their aims and concerns become indistinguishable in recognizing 'the challenge presented by Stalinism to truth and freedom' and the necessity of critiquing bureaucracy – whether of party or state.[19] The refusal to adhere to fixed positions, but rather to use knowledge to question belief, is one he attributes to Souyri – this has all the more poignancy because it echoes key aspects of Lyotard's own approach. Inevitably there is anachronism at work in this account of his friend and the politics they shared, but it is revealing that, despite the later Lyotard's differend with Marxism, he recognizes the importance of the lessons learned during this period, one he summarizes in relation to Souyri's approach to Marxism as follows:

> Far from offering to the mind the closed tranquillity of
> an established knowledge or a pragmatic guide, it was
> the proper name of his anxiety; it provided him all the
> opportunities to put again into question what he believed
> he had imagined, felt, known, and identified.[20]

This reflection anticipates Ramdani's recognition of the differends at work in Lyotard's writings on Algeria, as mentioned at the beginning of this chapter. It is the multiplicity of the differends which Lyotard and S. ou B. locate in the Algerian situation which results in an account of events that refuse to be simplified under the banner of a single cause, blind to the inconsistencies and contradictions of the events themselves.

The importance of Lyotard's writings on Algeria for Ramdani, writing in 1989 and informed by Lyotard's later writings on the differend, is Lyotard's insistence on recognizing the differends that exist between the colonizers and the colonized – their incompatible aims and irreconcilable attitudes to Algeria. The destruction of identities and cultures through the imposition and substitution of the language of the colonizer results in a wrong that cannot be recognized as such in a French court of law, under the hegemonic control of the colonizer. This is most clearly demonstrated by the repeated postponement of the granting of full citizenship to indigenous Algerians.

In his book *Lyotard and the Political*, James Williams draws attention to the importance of Ramdani's analysis of Lyotard, highlighting the three key versions of the differend which Ramdani puts forward: legal, linguistic and affective.[21] The differend resides between the colonizer and the colonized because of an incommensurability, a fundamental incompatibility, between the genres of discourse: the stake of the colonizer is economic – wanting the country to work for the interests of its (own) citizens, which fails to recognize the impact on the colonized – regardless of the loss of cultures, traditions, languages and nationality, an impact which belongs to 'the aesthetic regimen that expresses great suffering and loss'.[22] As briefly explained earlier, a differend is a conflict which cannot be resolved because of the lack of a means by which to judge fairly between two or more parties; in such situations, any judgement would wrong one party through the imposition of one genre of discourse and the consequent silencing of another. The term 'phrase' as used by Lyotard refers to many forms of communication and is not limited to linguistic phrases – silence is a phrase. Each phrase is constructed according to a set of rules – its regimen – which determines its form: showing, describing, questioning and so on. These regimens are not interchangeable but can be linked onto with specific aims – for example, showing is linked to description, and this linkage constitutes the genre of discourse and determines the aim of the resulting phrase. When a linkage is imposed, however, a conflict occurs; if a linkage wrongs the silenced, unarticulated phrase, it is a differend. Lyotard says that it is our task to bear witness to differends and seek to find a suitable idiom in which the differend can be expressed, hence the importance of paying attention to the affective response to events. As Williams explains,

> Affects have to be communicated, but they must also be created anew. What this means is that although the suffering and loss of the Algerian people demands a mode of communication that does not hide it in the all-pervasive language of the colonialist, the differend as affect also needs to be triggered in the outsider: it must be felt, in order to be recognised.[23]

It was this triggering of affect through aesthetics which later drew Lyotard to the importance of artistic examples and of the approach of a painter like Paul Cézanne, who struggles repeatedly, listening to that which has not yet been formed 'like the eye of a painter, freely sweeping across this contemporary reality', in contrast to the fixed viewpoint of blinkered political analyses.[24]

Lyotard's analysis is informed by his direct experiences in Constantine, writes Ramdani, which comes together with a non-dogmatic approach to Marxist critique, one which contrasts with many French intellectuals on the left at the time. Ramdani attacks Jean-Paul Sartre for his alleged Stalinism, critiquing his inability to see the war in Algeria as a unique event, as anything other than a possible stepping stone on the path to International

Socialism. The limitations of organizations in Algeria are similarly recognized. the Algerian Communist Party failing to ask questions of nationalism and the FLN ignoring questions of class and ethnic differences, developing a new class of exploiters within its ranks. The latter prompted questions which preoccupied Lyotard and the S. ou B. group greatly: should they support the FLN, despite its shortcomings as an organization which does not pursue the creation of a workers' democracy as its objective? Or was it their duty, given the 'flagrant' injustices they had witnessed, to support their struggle, despite their reservations, and in recognition of the contradictions which were exposed throughout the war?[25] Such contradictions and disagreements are central to all accounts of the workings of the group Socialisme ou Barbarie. It is this need to debate and work through the differends that Ramdani recognizes as an essential part of the process which gave rise to Lyotard's analysis of the war, and the struggles in Algeria.

3
Algeria and After

Why did Lyotard leave Algeria in 1952? During his two years in Constantine, Lyotard had made lasting friendships and become active in several union activities: he was *département* representative for the Union of Secondary Education, responsible for the study circle of the Confédération générale du travail (the largest French workers' union), in Constantine, and became involved in the *université populaire* (workers' university), set up by the historian and fellow *lycée* teacher André Nouschi. Lyotard's strong friendship with Pierre Souyri extended to both families and continued throughout their children's childhood: the Lyotards' second daughter, Corinne, was born in Algeria, as was Souyri's son. According to one of his students at the Lycée d'Aumale, Lyotard was a well-respected teacher who challenged his students with a taste of philosophical debates from Paris – Heidegger, Merleau-Ponty and Sartre – but also used aspects of Marxism to question their own positions on capitalism and colonialism. Drawing on memoirs written more than sixty years later, it is best to be cautious about the specificity of such accounts, yet Max Véga-Ritter, writing for the alumni association of the Lycée d'Aumale, mentions an absence of any tension within the group, which included students who would later become significant figures in the independent Algeria, declared a decade later in 1962. Among the thirty or so members of the philosophy class of 1950–51, three would later take up positions of power, including as President of the Algerian National Committee for Health, Ambassador

Lyotard (front row, centre) as Professeur de philosophie at the Lycée d'Aumale, Constantine, Algeria, 1950–51.

to Washington and Director of the National School of Algerian Administration. While André Nouschi's controversial work on the history of Algeria caused a stir – and sometimes embarrassment – Lyotard created similarly lively debates, demanding 'exercises of mental acrobatics'; the class was 'captivated by the personal charm, the clarity of exposition, the intelligence and the authenticity of our master's teaching'.[1] Véga-Ritter left Algeria to study English at the Sorbonne in 1952, and later became professor at Blaise Pascal University in Clermont-Ferrand. But why did Lyotard leave Algeria in 1952?

According to his elder daughter, the psychoanalyst Laurence Kahn, this is one of the last questions she asked Jean-François before he died: 'Why did we come back to France?' In 1952 there was evidence that war was on the horizon; Lyotard's political involvement was with not only the unions but the Algerian nationalists, and had they stayed there, he told her, he would have been involved with the liberation movements. Such an

involvement, however, would have exposed Andrée and his two
young daughters, Laurence and Corinne, as hostage targets.
For this reason, Lyotard took the decision to return to France,
where one of the first things he did was to establish contact
with the network which supported the Algerian separatists.

The need for secrecy regarding Lyotard's support for Algerian
nationalists was increased by his posting, after Constantine, to
the Prytanée military academy in La Flèche, near the city of Le
Mans in the Loire region of France. As with the École militaire
d'Autun, the Prytanée was run by the French department for
war, but it was a *lycée*, aimed at those training to be officers in
the French army. The move from Constantine to La Flèche seems
unusual, and the particular reason behind this posting is open
to conjecture. It could simply have been the first post available,
taken at a time when there was a sense of urgency to leave Algeria,
or was it a strategic posting on the part of the Inspector-General
of philosophy? The powerful position of Inspector-General,
responsible for the teaching of philosophy in *lycées* throughout
the French Republic, was held at the time by the formidable
Georges Canguilhem, best known for his work on the philosophy
of science and his influence on Michel Foucault, whose thesis on
the history of madness he was later to supervise. Canguilhem
had been involved in pacifist and anti-fascist groups before the
war and became active in the resistance: he was friends with Jean
Cavaillès, the philosopher of logic and mathematics executed by
a Nazi firing squad in 1944. Canguilhem would have been central
to Lyotard's first three appointments to Autun, Constantine and
La Flèche; perhaps Canguilhem recognized the value of placing a
philosophy teacher with a contrasting political view at the Prytanée.

Pierre Merlin, a pupil at the Prytanée from 1947 to 1957,
describes how the colonial wars in Indochina and Algeria were
part of their daily experience, whether through the funeral orations
for the latest young officer to be killed, or the talk by officers and

non-commissioned officers of their 'exploits', including acts of torture.[2] Merlin's view of the prevalent militarism was sceptical and while far from the norm among the pupils, he recalls that staff were by no means all political reactionaries. Pupils knew that Lyotard was on the left, but this was not remarkable – they were more concerned by the strictness of his teaching and the harshness of his marking. This had changed by the time of their later encounter at the experimental university centre at Vincennes, where Merlin was President from 1976 to 1980: Lyotard was known by then for his far left politics and a relaxed attitude to both teaching and marks.

Unlike most of the teachers at the military academy, the Lyotard family did not live in, or near, the Prytanée, but in a small HLM (council flat) near the station. The physical distance helped Lyotard to hide his political activities – including involvement with workers at the Renault factory in Le Mans and the networks supporting Algerian separatists – and his children knew not to speak of where he was, or where he had been. This secrecy was particularly important during the Algerian war, which extended through most of their time in La Flèche. The elder daughter, Laurence, recalls being invited to the home of a school friend, who turned out to be the daughter of a colonel at the Prytanée. She describes the sumptuous staircase of its interior and the short political lesson it provoked from her parents: they made it clear to her that she must never go there again, but play with friends from her own neighbourhood. Her parents feared the questions she might be asked and the risks of a return visit; to protect the family, a distance was kept between themselves and the Prytanée. This was just as well, as on another occasion when the sisters were playing hide and seek, they found an Algerian man hiding at the back of a *penderie* (walk-in cupboard) in their home, hidden there by their father when he had heard an unexpected knock at the door. Andrée May was fully aware of her husband's activities. She was a member of S. ou B. – which they joined together in 1954, having had an involvement

45

with the group since their return from Algeria – although she did not write for the journal, and family commitments limited her participation: 'the group made no allowances for child care,' writes Stephen Hastings-King, '. . . the mothers had to assume the role of "super mum", political activity was an additional demand.'[3] Although Jean-François and Andrée would visit the local group in Le Mans together, attendance at the editorial and assembly meetings in Paris would usually, during this period, be by Lyotard alone.

The Prytanée did have impressive historical antecedents: René Descartes had been a pupil during its former incarnation as the Jesuit Collège Henri IV, and more recent recruits to its teaching faculty included Henri Arvon, a German émigré of Jewish descent, who taught throughout Lyotard's seven years at Prytanée. Arvon was a specialist on the German philosopher Max Stirner, and wrote two volumes, *Le Bouddhisme* (Buddhism, 1951) and *L'Anarchisme* (Anarchism, 1951), for the popular pocket-book series *Que sais-je?*, founded by Paul Angoulvent at the Presses Universitaires de France during the Occupation. It was for this series that Lyotard wrote his first book, *La Phénomenologie* (Phenomenology), published in 1954, perhaps put forward by his former professor at the Sorbonne, Maurice de Gandillac. This small volume has remained in continual print since its first publication, and is an important indicator of Lyotard's philosophical position at this time, re-evaluating aspects of the phenomenological thought that was current in France during this period. Lyotard later explained that while studying at the Sorbonne, during the years 1946–8, he 'passed for a phenomenologist', although he felt he lacked the clear conviction of a philosophical position, unlike fellow students François Châtelet and Olivier Revault d'Allonnes, who, he recalls, called themselves Marxists.[4] In some ways, *Phenomenology* plays out a discussion between these two positions, particularly in its conclusion, yet for the most part it is an account of the ideas of Edmund Husserl, which are then contextualized by key thinkers associated with phenomenology in

France at that time – in particular, Merleau-Ponty, but also with references to Sartre, Martin Heidegger and an important interlocutor between phenomenology and Marxism, Trân Duc Thao. Thao was born in Vietnam, studied in Paris and returned to teach at the University of Hanoi in 1951, the same year his book *Phénoménologie et matérialisme dialectique* (Phenomenology and Dialectical Materialism) was published. Thao's book was clearly influential for Lyotard in his reflection on phenomenology as a critical philosophy; at its first mention, Lyotard adds the following remark in a footnote: 'I cannot recommend this remarkable little book too strongly to the reader.'[5] Thao's opinion is also used by Lyotard at a key point in his concluding remarks on the interrelationship between phenomenology, history and Marxism, a complex consideration which ultimately doubts the compatibility of the two.

In the bibliography to the first edition of *Phenomenology*, articles by Jean Wahl, Paul Ricoeur and Derrida are among those that accompany books on phenomenology in French: in addition to Thao's book, there was a recently published volume by Mikel Dufrenne in 1953, several by Merleau-Ponty including *Phenomenology of Perception* (1945), Sartre's *Being and Nothingness* (1943) and the study of Husserl by Emmanuel Levinas, *The Theory of Intuition in Husserl's Phenomenology* (1930). Levinas, who had attended the seminars of both Edmund Husserl and Heidegger in the late 1920s, was an important figure in promoting the discussion of the ideas of both these thinkers in France, and was to become an important focus for Lyotard's own later writings on questions of ethics. It is notable, however, that Lyotard's interest in Heidegger is considerably more reserved in *Phenomenology*.

After the war, scholars in France were aware of Heidegger's dubious political position, as rector of the university at Freiburg during the Nazis' rise to power and the war, but the consequences of this became the centre of a significant public debate in France in the 1980s. The debate was provoked by the publication of a dossier compiled by Victor Farías, which questioned the extent of Heidegger's complicity with the regime, his lack of comment on the events both before and after the war, and the impact on, or tainting of, his philosophy (and by implication those of his followers, a particularly strong tradition in France of which Derrida and Philippe Lacoue-Labarthe are two examples). Lyotard's complex contribution to this debate, published in 1988 as *Heidegger et 'les juifs'* (Heidegger and 'the jews'), related partly to Heidegger's silence in regard to his involvement with the Nazi party, but also addresses the question of forgetting, the immemorial and the process of returning to that which cannot be forgotten: anamnesis. In the context of this later book, Lyotard recalls that in 1947 he was part of a group of students chosen to visit Freiburg, where Heidegger had been elected rector in 1933. As part of a post-war rapprochement, two groups of French and German students worked together for a month. Though still traumatized by recent events, they 'sought a common understanding of their encounter in their trauma'.[6]

The French organizer of this visit was Jean Beaufret, the scholar most responsible for introducing Heidegger and his ideas to post-war France: it was his questions which prompted Heidegger to write *Lettre sur l'humanisme* (Letter on Humanism, 1946) and in 1955 Beaufret brought Heidegger to France for an important conference at Cerisy, which Sartre and Merleau-Ponty refused to attend because of the question over Heidegger's political associations during the war. Beaufret was influential – he taught *khâgne* at the Lycée Henri IV and prepared students for the *agrégation*. It was he who suggested that Lyotard and a small group of students should work together on this task – a group which comprised Léon-Louis Grateloup, Roger Laporte and Michel Butor, whose friendship and literary interests were to be significant for Lyotard. As for Lyotard's visit to Freiburg, it also involved a visit to Heidegger in his famous hut at Todtnauberg, and Lyotard is open about his own prejudice: 'I remember a sly peasant . . . of sententious speech and shifty eye, apparently lacking in shame and anxiety, protected by his knowledge and flattered by his disciple.' Despite prejudice and reservations, Lyotard adds, importantly, 'I continued to read his work.'[7]

It would be wrong, however, to suggest that Heidegger's place in *Phenomenology* is sidelined as a result of this personal hesitation on Lyotard's part. Aspects of *Being and Time* are discussed in *Phenomenology*, at a time when no full French translation was available, and, given the scope of the title, it is right that the first section is devoted to Heidegger's teacher, Husserl. In fact, as the philosopher Vincent Descombes wrote in 1979 (translated in 1980), the book gives a good summary of philosophical preoccupations in France in the 1950s, with phenomenological considerations having shifted from mathematics to the human sciences, and away from an anti-historical position to an engagement with Marxism.[8] This historical situating of Husserl's thought is striking in Lyotard's presentation: contextualizing the development of his work in relation to, and in resistance to, concerns of psychologism and pragmatism in late nineteenth- and early twentieth-century thought. The aim of *Phenomenology* is to consider the movement in relation to the history of philosophy and politics, bringing Husserl's method to bear on phenomenology and subsequently to address a critique of phenomenology brought by Marxism.

Published in the same year that Lyotard was accepted as a member of S. ou B., it is also possible to read the concluding sections of *Phenomenology* as an account of Lyotard's own decision to turn to a practical engagement in politics, to a militancy motivated by the active engagement of theory in practice: Marxist 'praxis'. In the short conclusion, Lyotard notes the political problem of phenomenology: 'It is not by chance that its right wing leans toward fascism, and that its "left" laughably contradicts itself.'[9] The accompanying footnote makes the references clear: works discussing Heidegger's politics, articles by Sartre and the disagreement played out between Sartre and one of the founders of S. ou B, Claude Lefort. Sartre's uncompromising support for the Communist Party is criticized by Lefort, as is the Stalinist tendency towards bureaucracy. In another article cited by Lyotard, Lefort's critique is supported by the other founder of S. ou B., Cornelius Castoriadis. Before returning to Lyotard's engagement with S. ou B., we will sketch out further some of the key points raised in *Phenomenology*, because it is in the complexity of Lyotard's assessment of the movement that we begin to gain a sense of that which draws him back to aspects of its method: it is not sufficient to say that this is Lyotard's rejection of phenomenology – there is no single phenomenological position any more than there is a single Marxist position.

What appeals to Lyotard in his reading of Husserl, as evidenced in *Phenomenology*, is his openness to contestation and the continual re-evaluation and questioning of truths. The phenomenology of Husserl is most famous for the consideration of that which appears to consciousness, 'given' without premeditated hypotheses or a link to that of which it is a phenomenon, hence the return to 'the things themselves', in order for the possibility that it might be otherwise considered. Husserl's point of departure is 'the immediate data of knowledge', but without recourse to categorical assumptions, the a priori approach of Immanuel Kant.[10]

It is this reflective approach without presuppositions, highlighted in Lyotard's introduction, that resonates with many of Lyotard's later writings, including his detailed, if somewhat unorthodox, considerations of Kant. Similarly, when Lyotard refutes the compulsion to explain phenomena, we can hear echoes of the future concern with event and that which is no longer the same once it is brought under consideration by thought: 'presence' was alluded to in this manner in the introduction, and there will be reiterations of similar concerns in the chapters to come. Introducing the English translation of

1991, Gayle Ormiston describes the work as a reflection on the philosophical project itself: 'a work *on* and *of* phenomenology', which draws attention to the fact that phenomenology itself is always in process, allowing Lyotard to embrace the ambiguities and the 'mutation' he describes as taking place, for example, between Husserl and Heidegger.[11] Of his task, Lyotard states, 'Our exposé will not attempt to erase this ambiguity, inscribed as it is in the very history of the phenomenological school.'[12]

Part of this history is the interrelationship of phenomenology with the human sciences – psychology, sociology and history – in order to consider that data is given to consciousness not in isolation, as the internalized subjectivity of Descartes' meditations, but to a consciousness that must be in relation to the world: 'interwoven with' and 'being-in' the world. This refusal to distinguish subject from object comes from the influence of Franz Brentano's intentionality on Husserl, the insistence that consciousness is always consciousness of something, and the necessity to describe the manner in which an object exists for me. In the section 'Phenomenology and History', Lyotard turns to Heidegger's example of a piece of antique furniture as a historical object which is woven into a multiplicity of subjective experiences – 'the "world" of which it is a part' – yet which exists for the consciousness as 'a flux of experiences, which are all in the present'.[13] History is not graspable as an object; it is not fixed by rules, but exists as a network of intentionalities. Consequently, it is through this network that the historian arrives at a meaning that is always 'in process', through that which Merleau-Ponty identified as purposive memory. This does not invalidate history – in fact, history remains central to Husserl's concept of truth:

this truth is not an atemporal and transcendent object,
but is experienced in the flux of becoming and will
be corrected indefinitely by other experiences.[14]

The resulting contingency, however, posed problems for the relationship of phenomenology to Marxism and a Marxist conception of history.

When reading the closing sections of *Phenomenology*, it is necessary to take care to identify that while Lyotard asserts that there can be no 'serious reconciliation' between phenomenology and Marxism, there are significant contributions that the former can make to the latter – specifically, regarding the attitude to ideology.[15] Indicating examples in the work of both Thao and Merleau-Ponty, Lyotard explains how the phenomenological approach to consciousness allows ideology to be interpreted neither as an illusion nor as an appearance, but in the lived experience of its existence: 'Ideology (in the general sense of the term) . . . is a reality just like the infrastructure itself.'[16] Ideology, as part of infrastructure, is integral to the forces of conflict that, according to the Marxist conception of history, drive change. Through the refocusing on a lived experience, the strictures of theory are questioned, according to Thao; Lyotard writes, 'Marx's theory is not a dogma, but a guide for action.'[17]

The form which this action took was to be a central preoccupation for Lyotard throughout the 1950s and '60s, and while his position changes with regards to Marx, the battle against the dogma of theory is one thread that continues to run throughout his work. Responding to Souyri's taunt that philosophers 'do no more than state problems', Lyotard embarked with Souyri on the detailed investigation of the 'most irrational of historical effects', undertaking situational analyses which necessitated an abandonment of the 'presumption of intelligence to speak of everything to everyone'.[18] When Jean-François and Andrée Lyotard, together with Pierre and Mireille Souyri, were accepted as members of Socialisme ou Barbarie in 1954, it was a small group which published a journal of the same name; originating as an oppositional group in 1946 within the Trotskyist Fourth International, it was initially known as the Chaulieu–Montal tendency, after the pseudonyms of its two leaders: Castoriadis (Chaulieu) and Lefort (Montal). Their disagreement with the International Communist Party came from their belief that revolution should come from the creative participation of the workers, not from the bureaucratic powers of an autonomous party, the intelligensia: while the Trotskyists criticized Stalinism, S. ou B. also criticized aspects of Leninism and its emphasis on the power of the party.

Part of the new influx of members who reinvigorated the group in the early 1950s was Daniel Mothé, the pseudonym of Jacques Gautrat, a worker at the Renault factory in Billancourt on the outskirts of Paris, and the worker who contributed most regularly to the journal and the discussions of the group. Mothé not only gave a worker's credibility to the group, which was sometimes dominated by more academic members, but an important connection to the Renault factory itself. As most industrial sites in France were, the Renault factory was dominated by the CGT union, which was closely allied to the French Communist Party (PCF), itself dominated by Stalinist tendencies and with little independence from the dictates of the Soviet Union. The interpretation of Marxism given by the PCF was the stranglehold against which many small Marxist groups fought in this period: Mothé and Gaspard (the pseudonym of Raymond Hirzel) distributed the typed, mimeographed, newsletter *Tribune ouvrière* in the factory, and later *Pouvoir Ouvrier*; both aimed to give a voice to the experiences of the workers, an analysis of which was integral to the approach of S. ou B.

Central to the understanding of the group was the need to reconsider Marxism in the light of contemporary events. The famous challenge from Lenin's *What Is to Be Done?* – 'Without revolutionary theory, no revolutionary action' – was adapted by Castoriadis: 'Without *development* of revolutionary theory, no development of revolutionary action.'[19] The simultaneous consideration of theory and practice as an ongoing engagement with socio-economic situations still 'in process' chimes clearly with Lyotard's assessment given in *Phenomenology*. S. ou B. had an impact in several ways through the 1950s and '60s, particularly in offering alternatives to the dogmatism of the French Communist Party, although the circulation of its publication never exceeded one thousand copies.[20]

Lyotard's first published contribution to the journal *S. ou B.* appeared in issue 18, January/March 1956, under the pseudonym F. Laborde and titled 'La Situation en Afrique du Nord' (The Situation in North Africa). It was followed by a dozen further articles over the next eight years, throughout the duration of the Algerian War. As both Castoriadis and Lyotard made clear, the articles that appeared in *S. ou B.* were collective undertakings and the result of 'discussions, dissections and debate' within the group.[21]

One of the most significant debates for Lyotard and S. ou B. concerned the practical engagement of the group and its role in supporting worker-organized activities, creating the opportunity for workers' experiences to affect those militating for socialism while simultaneously acknowledging the ideological impact of both the dominance of Communist Party ideologies and bourgeois attitudes among many of the workers themselves. *Pouvoir Ouvrier*, published from 1958, was part of this attempt to engage with workers directly, to give them the opportunity to contribute to a monthly publication which aimed at foregrounding the concrete experiences of workers, not only to assimilate 'the revolutionary ideology by the working class', as Mothé wrote in 1955, but as 'an assimilation of the workers' experiences by the revolutionary activists'.[22]

The other pressing, practical issue in which Lyotard was involved, and which caused dissension within the membership of S. ou B., was his involvement in the support networks for the Algerian independence movements. There is very little written about Lyotard's involvement in this network, partly due to the inherently secret nature of its activities, but in an interview in the late 1980s, Lyotard named his involvement as having been with the network led by the Egyptian militant communist Henri Curiel.[23] Curiel was an ally of the philosopher Francis Jeanson, who argued vehemently for Algerian nationalism and orchestrated, from 1957, practical support for the cause on the French mainland. Known as the *réseau Jeanson,* the network coordinated the distribution of funds and false papers to nationalists in Algeria, and shelter for those wanted by the French police. The activities of its supporters, known as the 'suitcase handlers' (*porteurs de valises*), became publicized following the arrest of seventeen members and six Algerians in February 1960, and their subsequent trial. Although Curiel was an ally of Jeanson and led the network while Jeanson was in hiding, he did not support Jeanson's beliefs that the Algerian struggle was a peasant revolution which could connect to the workers' movement in France, a hope he regarded as utopian.[24] The pragmatic vision of Curiel, whom Lyotard met only once, is closer to that expressed in Lyotard's own reports on the Algerian situation for S. ou B., and his decision to support the FLN in spite of its political shortcomings.

There were many discussions within S. ou B. regarding the ideological implication of supporting the FLN, and Lyotard was openly critical of the group's tactics in several articles. However, it was his practical support which, for pragmatic reasons, concerned members. There was a fear that his role as a *porteur de valises* endangered other members of the group, especially those who were foreign nationals. If Lyotard was caught, the security of the whole group would be endangered and members such as Alberto Véga and Castoriadis would be at risk of deportation. S. ou B. member Martine Vidal recalls that Lyotard arranged for representatives of the FLN to visit a closed meeting of S. ou B., in the hope that their position would be better understood. There was little discussion, however, as all they wanted to know was whether they would 'carry the cases'.[25]

There were many internal disputes within S. ou B., in part a result of the desire to ask questions at every turn, rather than being straitjacketed by rules or bureaucratic shackles; in 1958 Lefort and others left the group over questions of revolutionary organization, and a further scission was provoked by Castoriadis' increasing rejection of Marx's economic model. In 1963–4 the group split: Lyotard, Souyri and Véga led a breakaway which took the name of the monthly newspaper, *Pouvoir Ouvrier*, while those loyal to Castoriadis continued as S. ou B., until the suspension of the journal's publication with its fortieth issue in 1965. As Lyotard later reflected, he had perhaps sided with Souyri and the old-Marxist tendency out of loyalty, even though he had sympathy with Castoriadis' position at a time when his own suspicions about Marx were growing. Lyotard finally left P. O. in 1966, though his active political involvement was to be fired up again by the events of 1968, while he was teaching in the Faculty of Letters at Nanterre.

4

1968

It is April 2015. I am sitting in one of the most ancient parts of the Sorbonne listening to academics who knew Lyotard, who were his friends, colleagues and family. I listen to their disagreements about the different ways in which his work can be divided into periods: are there five or three? This lack of consensus is awkward and exciting. For some, the years of political engagement constitute a first period; for others, they are the bedrock of his philosophical writings which never turn away from politics. However, each narrative acknowledges the role of his active political militancy, which often remains under-acknowledged in the English-speaking world. Yet this discussion takes place in the Sorbonne, still a bastion of the establishment against which students famously fought in 1968.

For ease of understanding, we often benefit from the process of periodization – early, middle and late – whether describing artists, writers or philosophers. Yet there are always anachronic interventions which disturb and distort – revisions, repetitions and feedback loops. Lyotard's work is both a good example of this disrupted narrative and a commentary on it, be it in the writings on the postmodern or the complications to sequential linear temporality indicated as event or anamnesis. One debate about periodizing Lyotard's work came, initially, from a research project, led by Jean-Michel Salanskis, at the University of Nanterre in 2008. Lyotard had taught at Nanterre in 1968; there he played an important role in *Mouvement du 22 mars* (March 22 Movement) and the events of May that followed. Forty years later, Salanskis' seminar for doctoral philosophy students was on Lyotard's work; he introduced the seminar and the resulting publication with an account of five broadly chronological periods, beginning with the politics of S. ou B. and traversing *Discours, figure*, 1971 (Discourse, Figure, 2011); *Économie libidinale*, 1974 (Libidinal Economy, 1993) and *Le Différend*, 1983 (The Differend, 1988); a last period relates to *l'enfance* (childhood) and *La phrase-affect* (the affect-phrase).[1]

This present book makes no claims for a particular periodization, and while it follows a trajectory that is broadly similar to that outlined by Salanskis, it gives a greater emphasis to texts and activities beyond the 'major' philosophical books, thereby foregrounding the breadth of Lyotard's interests. In addition, there are twists and turns which do not fit a neat chronology – the result, in part, of the chequered history of publication. We have encountered already, in Chapter Two, the late collection of Lyotard's political writings (*La Guerre d'Algériens*, 1989; *Political Writings*, 1993), and I have included above the comparative French and English publication dates of the three main books in order to highlight the parallel chronology of Lyotard's work in English translation. Publication dates are important in terms of igniting debate and commentary but also come with a warning not to neglect the context in which the writing was undertaken. This is particularly important as this chapter moves through the 1960s to the publication of Lyotard's Doctorat d'État, *Discours, figure*, in 1971; it represents the culmination of many years of research together with a reconsideration of the phenomenology which had formed the focus of his first book. One of the reasons Lyotard resisted writing the book for so long, he explains, was a 'fear of being seduced . . . mesmerized by language', with the risk of being distracted from its goal – 'the practical critique of ideology'. The present book is itself nothing more than a detour (*détour*) on the way to this critique.[2]

'Sois jeune et tais-toi' (Be young and shut up), Atelier Populaire, Paris, May 1968.

The value of such a critique will soon be thoroughly attacked in his subsequent work, but the reference to *détour* evokes the strategic reversal of power in the language of May '68 and emphasizes the political context in which *Discourse, Figure* was written.

When Lyotard defended his thesis for the Doctorat d'État in 1971, two members of the panel were former fellow students from his time as a student at the Sorbonne: Gilles Deleuze and Michel Butor. The textual arrangements of examples of Butor's work are given careful consideration in the latter part of *Discourse, Figure*, one of the few contemporary artistic references in a work with a long historical reach including illuminated manuscripts, paintings of Duccio and Masaccio, and works by Paul Klee. Butor's texts refuse to conform to the codes of either text or image, rather oscillating between the two through a mobility that Lyotard had identified in the earlier examples: a subversive power which at once opens and challenges the mind. Five years later, Michel Butor's poetic contribution to the special Lyotard edition of the journal *L'Arc* in 1976 is punctuated by the refrain '*Nous moquant des autorités*' (We are mocking the authorities). Between these refrains, Butor remembers his visit to Lyotard at La Flèche:

> Stones and hearts were broken in that town of La
> Flèche with its Prytanée. Where you survived among
> the military and their apprentices whilst I scribbled
> at your desk the first lines of *L'Emploi du temps*.[3]

Rewriting the account in prose for *Yale French Studies* in 2001, Butor is very clear: 'He was very unhappy there.' The account is softened by the following vignette, however: 'I brought him a vinyl record of *The Musical Offering* and, in the evening, we would listen to Scarlatti Sonatas.'[4] The circularity of Bach's fugues and the passage and re-passage of time in Butor's *L'Emploi du temps* (Passing Time) form a useful accompaniment to Lyotard's changing circumstances: breaking away from La Flèche to teach at the Sorbonne in 1959–66, and then moving to the less stifling environment of the new faculty at Nanterre. It is to Nanterre that Butor's recollections jump next, describing how Lyotard's 'role was fundamental in the student mobilization'; Butor wrote the poems *Tourmente* (Turmoil) with the idea that Lyotard would give them to his 'angry students': he hoped they would be written on blackboards, such was the artistic fervour of this utopia in creation.[5]

On moving to Paris in 1959 and starting to teach at the Sorbonne, Lyotard found himself surrounded by young people who had an open dissatisfaction with the current political system, not least the recall of those who had already undertaken military service. Events in Algeria had prompted de Gaulle's return to power after twelve years in the political wilderness, and while his declaration made in Algiers in June 1958, *Je vous ai compris* ('I have understood you'), was interpreted by the Algerian French as a sign of support, he made the first moves towards a separation of Algeria from France. The referendum of September 1958 on de Gaulle's proposed constitution for a new Fifth Republic provoked further political divisions: Pierre Vidal-Naquet, for example, recalls his surprise that some of those who had campaigned alongside him to expose the use of torture by French forces in Algeria joined the 78 per cent who voted for de Gaulle. Lyotard, however, had nothing but scepticism regarding either the aims of the state or the lengths to which its operatives would go to maintain power. In *S. ou B.* (no. 29), Lyotard wrote of the missed opportunity offered by the crisis of the Fourth Republic for the revolutionary Left: instead, the Fifth Republic was born out of the '*depoliticization* of the exploited classes', their disillusionment.[6]

Lyotard's influence in S. ou B. grew significantly with his move to Paris: not only was he reporting on the most pressing political issue of the day – Algeria – but he was able to recruit new members. In the early 1960s, Lyotard taught the *propédeutique* (propaedeutic) – the first year of students enrolling to arts and science courses – which meant he was exposed to large numbers of students; for several members of S. ou B., it was an encounter with the charm and intelligence of Lyotard which drew them to the group.[7] In 1957 the number of full, paid-up militants was fewer than twenty; by the spring of 1961 this had grown to 87 (44 of whom were in Paris). A recently published memoir by Sébastian de Diesbach, a young militant with the group

throughout this period, gives a description of Lyotard at
this time:

> as thin as a rake, a slim, brilliant, totally honest man. He
> listened to you intently, without interrupting, leaving you
> to finish, and then summarized your words better than
> you would have been able to. You were strutting about,
> before the dismay of hearing him destroy, piece by piece,
> the reasoning of which you had once been so proud.[8]

Lyotard's involvement in the group was known much more widely
in Paris than had been the case in La Flèche and his involvement
in the publication of *Pouvoir Ouvrier* gave him some autonomy to
pursue an engagement that was distinct from that of Castoriadis.
Correspondence between Lyotard and Sorbonne professor Maurice
de Gandillac makes it clear that Gandillac – who is likely to have
had a role in his appointment – was aware of Lyotard's 'unofficial'
activities; from 1960 Lyotard no longer used a pseudonym when
writing for *S. ou B.*, although caution remained necessary with
regard to his involvement in the support for Algerian independence,
as demonstrated by the trials of the Jeanson network and the arrest
of Curiel in 1960.

The lectures given to the propaedeutic class of 1964 were published
in 2012 as *Pourquoi philosopher?* (Why Philosophize?, 2013), with a
contextualizing introduction by Lyotard's younger daughter, Corinne
Enaudeau. She writes that his political, philosophical and teaching
activities are interwoven, provoked by the need to ask questions and
driven by the lack which provokes the act of philosophizing itself:

> His conviction, as early as 1964, was that you can be
> inoculated with a grain of philosophy only if you let
> yourself be haunted by absence and find the paradoxical
> energy to contaminate others with it, to tell them about

the 'law of debt', the debit that can never be paid off.
His work enabled this grain to spread and grow . . . [9]

Enaudeau identifies in Lyotard's approach the need to unlearn what
one already thinks one knows. In 1964, the year Lyotard and Souyri
split from S. ou B. to form P. O. as a separate group, this meant the
need to unlearn his reliance on the Marxist hope for revolution
and a history of resolution, while maintaining the need to attest
to the presence of exploitation, which had been the mainstay of
his writings on Algeria. Lyotard's writings for *S. ou B.* made it clear
that the Algerian situation could not fit into a pre-existing Marxist
schema and while Lyotard had never been under the illusion that
a workers' revolution in Algeria was a possibility, the independent
Algeria that emerged in 1962 confirmed his worst fears: a power
vacuum created in the wake of the 'shock' of decolonization, the
mass emigration of the pieds noirs and an economic crisis which
pre-empted further political turmoil and the 1965 *coup d'état*.

   The question of Marxist engagement which concerned Lyotard
at the end of *Phenomenology* in 1954 is still evident in his lectures
ten years later, most explicitly in the fourth and final lecture,
titled 'On Philosophy and Action'. Taking Marx's famous early
aphorism from *Theses on Feuerbach* – 'Philosophers have merely
interpreted the world in different ways; the point is to change
it' – as his point for discussion, Lyotard follows the tradition
of S. ou B. in emphasizing the role that speaking can have in
acting to transform reality, in contrast to those who appear to
act while only in fact maintaining the status quo. Speaking can
gather up and give voice to a latent meaning, 'in the wave of
mute communication' (of which Merleau-Ponty writes in *Signs*)
in order that action might be reciprocal – not the result of an
infallible politics but one which acknowledges that 'doing also
means allowing oneself to be done to' – and that laws might be
rewritten and reinvented as part of this transformation.[10] There

is no single meaning of history and society, no fixed end in revolution and resolution – 'Nothing can be taken for granted.'[11]

Lyotard's consideration of Marx's thinking did not end here; it did not even end with the decisive and explosive break declared by his book *Libidinal Economy* of 1974, but his relationship shifted to such an extent that when Lyotard attacks the unwavering adhesion to the orthodox ideology of the Communist Party, it is sometimes wrongly assumed that Marx's thought is always an integral part of the target. Lyotard's break was with the exclusivity of Marxist thought as the only framework through which to consider social and political problems. The personal consequences of his final break with P. O. in 1966 were significant, and while his friendship with Souyri continued, they had lost their shared belief in the common language of Marxism.

A similar difficulty awaited Lyotard's first attempts to undertake research towards the Doctorat d'État, a higher doctorate similar to the present *habilitation*, needed to supervise research students and to progress up the academic hierarchy. In taking the position of *maître-assistant* at the Sorbonne, it was expected that Lyotard would embark on a programme of research. He registered a thesis under the supervision of Paul Ricoeur with the title *Structure et histoire* (Structure and History), for which extensive plans and notes exist (dated 1964–7), some of which are written on the backs of flyers for Pouvoir Ouvrier and the Union of Teachers in Higher Education. Soon after his move to Nanterre, however, his focus had shifted towards aesthetics, while maintaining a critique of structuralist approaches. Ricoeur's role in building the philosophy department at Nanterre had enabled him to appoint both Levinas and Dufrenne to the faculty. With his interest in both aesthetics and phenomenology, it was Dufrenne who was best suited to take over the supervision of Lyotard's new research, which would become *Discourse, Figure*, although the presence of Levinas' thought is a significant one which would become manifest in several texts in the late 1970s, culminating in the explicit consideration of ethical phrases in *The Differend*.[12]

The political desire for economic development accompanied a dramatic expansion of higher education during the 1960s. The antiquated, authoritarian systems received few reforms, however, and initiatives such as the founding of Nanterre in 1964 highlighted existing limitations in the system: it was over-centralized, lacking in student representation and adhered to outdated disciplinary boundaries. Nanterre was far removed from the Sorbonne socially and economically: the location of the new campus was close to shanty towns (*bidonvilles*) occupied by immigrant workers and areas of social housing (HLM). When Ricoeur arrived with Pierre Grappin, the appointed dean, to lay the foundation stone, the taxi driver refused to drive onto the site for fear of becoming stuck in the mud. Later, when Henri Lefebvre – who led the department of sociology – was asked why the May '68 uprisings started in Nanterre, he replied, 'to answer the question one should look outside the window', indicating the poverty of the surroundings.[13] The first intake of arts and social science students numbered 2,872 in 1964 and grew year-on-year to reach 11,400 in 1967, a number for which the faculty was ill prepared, provoking a strike in the first term which was followed by frequent unrest and demonstrations in the second.

Ricoeur welcomed educational reform: he expressed the need for such in an interview with the journal *Esprit*, published in 1964, describing the situation as 'explosive' and on the point of crisis. His own vision was informed in part by his experiences of teaching in Chicago and the U.S. tradition of liberal arts education, an irony which did not escape those commentators opposed to the 'American imperialism' evidenced by contemporary television reports of the Vietnam War. In 1964 Lyotard also published a bitter critique of the education system, in the student journal of the Sorbonne – its title 'Dead Letter' refers to the state of the Faculty of Letters:

At the Sorbonne one does not procreate, one does not love, one is not a body, one neither eats nor dies, one does not work (in the sense of the workshop). The mind alone seems able to earn the right of entry; but the mind is simply the meaning of what is left behind at the door, left outside.[14]

Early in 1966 Lyotard wrote to Gandillac, explaining his decision to follow Ricoeur to Nanterre. Gandillac's response expresses no surprise, simply an acknowledgement that the new faculty would provide a more lively and sympathetic milieu.[15]

Much has been written about the stages leading up to the events of May 1968. This culminated in a month of explosive expressions of dissatisfaction with the state, de Gaulle and the capitalist system in general from students, teachers and workers. At its height, an estimated ten million were on strike across France: universities and factories were occupied; workers' control was widely discussed and action committees put new forms of organization into practice. Lyotard was heavily involved in the March 22 Movement, famously fronted by Daniel Cohn-Bendit, first at Nanterre and then in the Latin Quarter and beyond. While the media chose to focus on individuals such as Cohn-Bendit and leaders of the student and teaching unions (Alain Geismar and Jacques Sauvageot), the collaborative nature of the groups that supported and coordinated the largely spontaneous events, meetings, marches and demonstrations in the spring of 1968 would make it difficult, if not futile, to isolate Lyotard's role. It is sufficient to say that he was an active participant: Vidal-Naquet comments on a March 22 leaflet that was 'more or less drafted by Lyotard'; he spoke; he wrote; he marched along with thousands of others.[16] There were multiple and diverse influences on the movement: Cohn-Bendit's book *Obsolete Communism* borrowed liberally from *S. ou B.* – 'readers . . . will appreciate how much this book owes to them [S. ou B.]'; the situationists and Guy Debord,

'Votre Lutte est la nôtre!' (Your struggle is ours!) March 22 Movement leaflet, 24 May 1968. Lyotard refers to his involvement in writing of this tract in *Peregrinations*.

briefly an S. ou B. member, were a significant influence, although Lefebvre disputes the extent of their role – 'they were not the animators' – while also acknowledging that he encouraged the early rebelliousness of his sociology students: 'I stirred things up a bit.'[17] Cohn-Bendit and Jean-Pierre Duteuil rejected the idea that any one writer was the inspiration – the impetus came from many sources: televised global events and discussions on the street, ineffective educational reforms and unemployment.[18] Such is the melee of '68 and its mythology, but its impact for Lyotard was transformative.

In the lectures of 1964 Lyotard had called to students to be open to change and transformation: 'doing also means allowing oneself to be done to'.[19] The experience of participation in the events of 1968 affected Lyotard greatly. It re-energized both his thinking and his politics, once more giving him a sense of collective endeavour, similar to that which S. ou B. had once given him, but now with an emphasis on the political connections between art and politics. This was to remain an integral part of his thinking. In 'Dead letter', Lyotard had written that 'Culture is lending an ear to what strives to be said, culture is giving a voice to those who do not have a voice and who seek one.'[20] In *Discourse, Figure*, the same theme is developed: 'What cannot be tamed is art as silence.'[21] Here it is also possible to identify the preoccupations which will take an ethical turn in the defence of that which cannot be voiced, both in *The Differend* and in the later return to art, literature and music as that which bears witness to the differend, to presence and to that which cannot be verbalized (referred to in an important late essay as the 'affect-phrase'). Wanting to draw out these threads of continuity, without suggesting that Lyotard is always presenting the same argument, is analogous to one of the main problems presented by *Discourse, Figure* – acknowledging that modes of presentation not only repress alternatives but feed off the power of difference evidenced by the incompatible, heterogenous realms of discourse and figure.

Discourse, Figure is at once difficult, complex, rich and rewarding; it is one of the major philosophical works from this period but has received relatively little attention. The organization of the book is itself a working-through of its concerns. Beginning with a critique of structuralist linguistics, Lyotard uses phenomenological arguments to open up the restrictions of a philosophy of language based on opposition, to difference, introduced by Merleau-Ponty's emphasis on the sensuousness of the visual field and the mobility of the eye. The limitations of phenomenology as an analysis of conscious perception, however, are then critiqued through a turn to the primary processes of the unconscious and the approach of 'free floating attention', taken from Freud's working method, allowing the power of psychic negation to be recognized and the work of desire to destabilize attempts at systematization. Such a description of the book as a series of substitutions, however, fails to describe the ways in which these different plates slide over one another to enable tectonic collisions to occur, frequently made manifest through detailed discussions of painting, poems, the philosophy of language and complex readings of Freud's texts. In his introduction to Lyotard's work (1991), Bill Readings gives an extensive account of *Discourse, Figure* in relation to literary criticism, remarking, 'Rather than an account, Lyotard demands from us a *performance, a work.*'[22] In reviewing the English translation of *Discours, figure* for the journal *Art History* in 2013, I followed Readings's advice and, listening to the demand being made, wrote as follows:

> There is an image by Penny Slinger, a photo-collage showing an ear placed inside an open mouth; the earlobe overlaps the lower lip, highlighting a single pearl earring. It is charged with eroticism: I trace my tongue around its contours and come to rest on the tiny smooth sphere, which challenges me then to speak. This is not an illustration but a provocation, one which comes to mind as I read the opening challenges laid down by Lyotard in *Discourse, Figure*: 'One does not read or understand a picture. Sitting at the table one identifies and recognizes linguistic units; standing in representation one seeks out plastic events. Libidinal events.' You can search for the Penny Slinger image now, on your laptop, but it will not be a single image: it is already crowded with others – and even when it is facing you it is framed by a digital distance that lessens its confrontational impact. You are reading it now and have missed the lip-smacking

'mmmm' which makes the eye jump. I have a colleague who talks to students in such guttural terms – 'look at this . . . mmm . . . tschm tschm tschmm, don't you want to taste it?' she entices, embarrassing them into eating with their eyes. Why does she use her mouth for other-than-speech? It is to open up the body to that phenomenological experience of sensation which makes the eye dance, the colour sing; and yet we know such aesthetic indulgences have no radical potential, no social import, no political impact. Don't we?[23]

In his introduction to the English edition of *Discours, figure*, John Mowitt listens to the sparse presence of Marx in *Discourse, Figure* and asks whether what is really struggling to be heard is an attempt to think the possibility of a non-dialectical Marxism? Marx's *Critique of Hegel's 'Philosophy of Right'* figures in the section 'opposition and difference' as part of a wider discussion of the role of negation, central to Lyotard's reading of Freud, in order to explain that 'actual extremes cannot be mediated with each other precisely because they are actual extremes . . . they neither need nor complement one another.'[24] This discussion opens up, for Lyotard, the possibility of thinking a relation of difference that is prompted by unconscious desire, not the opposition of complementarities easily inscribed into a totality by a Hegelian dialectics, but that extreme which the system – whether language or thought – cannot bear, except as 'an unredeemable violence . . . that can find no place in the conscious order of legitimacy'.[25] For Lyotard, it suggests

the possibility to think a relation through without including it in a system of oppositions; in other words, insofar as thinking and placing the object in such a system are one and the same operation, the possibility to think a relation through without thinking it.[26]

In his acknowledgements at the start of *Discours, figure* Lyotard thanks the participants of the course and seminar he taught at Nanterre in 1967–8 and 1968–9 respectively. Salanskis was a student in the class that began in autumn 1968 after the real possibility of revolution, which some had felt in May, had been stymied by the concessions drawn by the unions on working conditions, social security benefits and trade union rights. The reformists had worked within the system and maintained their own power base; de Gaulle had called elections and achieved a majority in the second round of ballots in June, only to leave the Élysée the following year having been defeated in a referendum. For Lyotard, however, the struggle continued. Salanskis recalls, 'At the start of term, September 1968, Jean-François Lyotard told us of the newness, the novelty [*la nouveauté*] of what had come to pass', urging students not to jump to conclusions, or to read the events as mirroring previous occurrences, but to listen to the 'word or gesture of desire' in the 'unpredictable and insane "mobilization"' of which they were a part.[27]

It is the same radical refusal of systematization that leads to a valorization of the figural at the outset of *Discourse, Figure* while identifying the interweaving of the figural at the heart of discourse – not as its opposite, but integral to it, through its resistance. The political tenor and implications of *Discourse, Figure* are made more apparent in the essays collected as *Dérive à partir de Marx et Freud* (Casting Adrift from Marx and Freud), which in its edition of 1973 makes the presence of Marx much more explicit. In the wake of 1968, Lyotard witnessed a 'resurgence of Stalinism' and the need once more to critique the conservatism of the 'Communist' Party – indicating his scepticism with scare quotes – together with the increasingly influential readings of Marx by Louis Althusser at the École Normale Supérieure.[28] The long, untranslated essay published in *Dérive*, 'La Place de l'aliénation dans le retournement marxiste', critiques Althusser's lack of attention to Marx's concept of alienation, and while Lyotard shows respect for Althusser's thinking in many places, sharing as they do a critique of Hegelian dialecticism, the separation of later Marx from early Marx will become the object of persistent ridicule through the characters of 'Old Prosecutor Marx' and 'Little Girl Marx' in *Libidinal Economy.*

5

Dérive

'Something is always happening in the arts . . . which incandesces the embers glowing in the depths of society.'[1] This validation of artistic creativity as the workshop for new ideas is not a 'comfortable retreat, but the fault and fracture giving access to the subsoil of the political scene'.[2] Thus explains Lyotard in the introductory essay to the collection *Dérive à partir de Marx et Freud*, a collection of writings that is testament not only to the events of May 1968 and its aftermath, but to Lyotard's new and energetic engagement with the arts, as a workshop to 'forge critical concepts'. In 1964 he had criticized the Faculty of 'Dead Letters' at the Sorbonne, where 'one does not work (in the sense of the workshop)', for its neglect of the body, of the sexual, whereas in 1970 he spoke of how the student body, responding to an experience of alienation, was able to 'seriously challenge society'.[3]

The documents compiled in *Dérive* include political demands, discussions on Marxism and an active analysis of music, posters and psychoanalytic theory. Several of the pieces are the result of collaborative or collective undertakings: an interview for the art magazine *vh 101*; notes for a contribution to a student-initiated debate at Nanterre on 'Art and Society'; experimental writing created with collage; collaborative responses to the music of Luciano Berio and to the posters of May '68 (with Dominique Avron and Bruno Lemenuel), the latter undertaken as part of seminars at Nanterre. It is worth paying attention to the form and contents of this collection, not only because of the diversity of its subject-matter and approach, but because of the deliberate decision to include essays only from 1968 to 1970. The collection opens with *Préambule à une charte* (Preamble to a Charter) – demands proposed for university reforms and accepted by the student Action Committee in mid-June 1968 – and ends with *Le 23 mars* (March 23). A footnote to the title 'March 23' reads, 'Unpublished introduction to an unfinished book on the movement of March 22', which highlights Lyotard's refusal to historicize the events or make them fit into a 'system of knowledge', warning readers that no narrative should be expected, being a form that tends towards the fulfilment of a desire, with 'the function of drawing a "moral"', to make sense of history.[4] For Lyotard, it is the very lack of sense, the intensity of not knowing, which drove him to respect the events of 1968 as that which he would later term a 'sign of history', one that indicates the extension of the mind in a moment of enthusiasm for the intensity of the possibilities of the present.

Dérive à partir de Marx et Freud was published in 1973 in the 'S' series of 10/18 pocket paperbacks – a series directed by the young writer and art critic Bernard Lamarche-Vadel, who would also publish a second collection of Lyotard's writings in 1973, *Des dispositifs pulsionnels* – and include Lyotard's first long essay on a contemporary visual artist, Jacques Monory, in the collection *Figurations 1960/1973*. It was not unusual at this time for art to be the site of radical political discussion, as Lamarche-Vadel later reflected, 'I came from a generation for whom art was a thing of real struggle.'[5] The extent to which Lyotard's engagement with the arts is, in some ways, typical of the time is made clear in the study of 2010 by Sarah Wilson, *The Visual World of French Theory*, which considers the engagement of thinkers, including Lyotard, Foucault and Deleuze, but also Bourdieu and Althusser, alongside artists belonging to the loose grouping of Narrative

Kiff Bamford, drawing of Lyotard's 1973 collections, pencil on paper.

Figuration painters, about whom these five thinkers wrote at this time. What is less typical is the extent to which Lyotard continued this interest and engagement with the arts for the rest of his life, now made more visually evident by the six-volume edition *Jean-François Lyotard: Writings on Contemporary Art and Artists*, edited by Herman Parret with the University of Leuven Press. This project is a rich academic resource; making many previously untranslated and out-of-print texts available, it also demonstrates the breadth of Lyotard's interests. Lyotard wrote texts on more than twenty individual artists; co-curated the significant new media exhibition *Les Immatériaux* at the Centre Georges Pompidou, Paris, in 1985; and in 1987 devised a reflection on painting – *Que peindre?* (What to Paint?) – which specifically considers the work of Valerio Adami, Shusaku Arakawa and Daniel Buren, while also returning to some of the questions posed in *Discourse, Figure* more than fifteen years earlier.

What the finesse of the Leuven collection cannot hope to recreate, however, is the materiality of the earlier publications:

their diverse formats, modes of presentation and dissemination. The three 10/18 paperbacks were part of a response to the demand for new reading matter in the wake of '68, an appetite for the social sciences recognized by the publisher Christian Bourgois. It seems appropriate, then, that Lyotard's first book to appear in English, in 1984, would be in a series similarly popular with artists and students – and also measuring 10 x 18 cm (4 x 7 in.) – the Foreign Agents series by Semiotext(e). The editor of this book, *Driftworks*, was himself a foreign agent; having been a student of Lyotard's at Nanterre in 1966–9, Roger McKeon became involved in the New York-based Semiotext(e) collective in the mid-1970s at a time when Lyotard was beginning to teach frequently at several North American universities, including the University of California, San Diego, and Johns Hopkins University in Baltimore.

Lyotard's experiences as a 'travelling professor' played a significant role in his life, his work and the dissemination of his ideas, whether contemplating the cultural barrier of the *Pacific Wall* from the West Coast of the United States in his intervention into Michel Vachey's novel *Toil* in 1975, or the later sardonic reflections on the conventions of transcontinental academic visitation in 'Marie Goes to Japan' (1993):

> European Visiting Professors on campus are Greek tutors: slaves, freed slaves, dependents, wards of Rome, mercenaries of an Amerikapital that worries about its border areas.[6]

> A half hour at the hotel to freshen up. Sometimes, it's after eighteen hours of nonstop flying, huh? Cocktails and dinner, then the lecture and a drink. Or a cocktail and the lecture, then dinner. It's the same thing everywhere in all the cities of the world . . . At one in the morning, the hotel foyer is full of businessmen. They're making deals, in all the languages of the world. What the fuck are you doing here, Marie?[7]

The cynical reflections and hurried, harassed experiences of Marie contrast with the excitement offered by the years surrounding 1968, however, and while Lyotard may have gathered together some of the spirit of '68 in the *Dérive* collection by binding its contents to the years 1968–70, the second collection of 1973 *Des dispositifs pulsionnels* prepares for the intensities to come. The title refers directly to Freud, his description of the *Trieb* – *la pulsion* – the drive or instinct and the apparatus (*dispositif*) of which it is a part: in truth, the title presents no small difficulties of translation. What the title points to is the importance of Freud in Lyotard's thinking, as developed at the end of *Discourse, Figure* in relation to the figural force of desire that drives and disrupts forms of established discourse, named in *Des dispositifs pulsionnels* as the force or energy of Nietzsche's *Wille* (Will).

Lyotard's interest in Freud is as a philosopher; he had no time for, and less belief in, psychoanalysis as a practice – 'bullshit' was the impassioned argument he made against his elder daughter's decision to turn away from historical research with the renowned J-P Vernant to become a psychoanalyst.[8] One might also reflect on the irony that Castoriadis, the father figure of S. ou B. and one-time frequent household guest of the Lyotards, also retrained to become a psychoanalyst. Although Lyotard had made reference to Freud in his first book *Phenomenology*, it was largely through a reading of Merleau-Ponty. A more serious consideration of Freud was necessary in the early 1960s, when Ricoeur was his supervisor; Ricoeur's own work on Freud was published in 1965, but it was undoubtedly Jacques Lacan who was best known for his 're-reading' of Freud at this time.

Lacan came to international prominence in 1953 with his 'Rome Discourse', delivered as a report of his newly founded Societé Française de Psychanalyse (SFP), which argued for a structuralist reading of Freud, a 'return to Freud', as he named it; in the same year, he began to deliver his weekly seminars, which were to continue for the next 26 years. A complicated sequence of events forced Lacan to break from the SFP in 1963. 'Excommunicated', he founded the École freudienne de Paris, and in 1964 the seminars moved from the psychiatric hospital of Sainte-Anne to the École normale supérieure (ENS). This new location allowed for a larger audience, one that was more broadly philosophical and less specifically tied to the practice of psychoanalysis. Élisabeth Roudinesco's history of the period describes how the move to the ENS drew Althusser and his students to the seminars, commenting on the 'obvious analogy between the return to Freud theorized by Lacan . . . and Althusser's reading of Marx', the latter being published in the collective *Lire le Capital* (Reading Capital) and *Pour Marx* (For Marx) in 1965.[9] In addition to this 'cartel' of structuralist Marxists, which included a significant Maoist tendency, were those regular attendees who had been with Lacan since Sainte-Anne, including Serge Leclaire, although many significant followers had remained with the SFP, among them Jean Laplanche and Jean-Bertrand Pontalis. It was into this milieu that Lyotard entered in 1964–5, attending many of the seminars which were later published as *Les Quatre concepts fondamentaux de la psychanalyse* (The Four Fundamental Concepts of Psychoanalysis, or Seminar XI). In 1964, however, there were few written accounts of Lacan's thought; it was not until November 1966 that the first substantial collection of 35 assorted papers was finally published, simply as *Écrits*, which Lyotard read as soon as it was published.

Lyotard's most direct and critical response to Lacan comes in the section of *Discourse, Figure* titled 'The Dream-work Does not Think', which was published as an independent article in 1968 in the *Revue d'esthétique*, edited by Dufrenne. A detailed assessment of Freud's account of the process of dreamwork in *The Interpretation of Dreams*, Lyotard emphasizes the psychic process described by Freud as a model of the incoherent workings of the figural. As a direct refutation of Lacan's famous dictum 'the unconscious is structured like a language', Lyotard argues that

the 'language' of the unconscious is not modelled on
articulated discourse, which, as we know, finds utterance
according to a language. Rather, the dream is the acme
of the inarticulate, deconstructed discourse from
which no language, even normal, is entirely free.[10]

Dreamwork, particularly that of 'secondary revision', is given as an
example of that most extreme instance of the figural which Lyotard
names the 'figure-matrix': closest to the unconscious, it is driven by
desire and operates through blocking together incommensurable
realms (in this case the latent and manifest levels of dreamwork).
By emphasizing the figural at work in the process of dreamwork,
Lyotard takes issue with the application of Roman Jakobson's
structuralist interpretation of language by Lacan, insisting on
the 'radically unfulfilled nature of desire' which cannot fit into a
predetermined system of signification.[11] Lyotard is aware that he is
attacking not only the premise of Lacan's argument but 'the current
tendency to stuff all of semiology into linguistics', citing Roland
Barthes' *Éléments de sémiologie* (Elements of Semiology, 1964) as an
example and echoing his implied critique of Derrida, made earlier
in *Discourse, Figure*:

> One does not break free at all from metaphysics by placing
> language everywhere; on the contrary, one fulfils it, one
> enacts the repression of the sensory and of *jouissance*.[12]

Lyotard's critique is acknowledged by Lacan in the preface to the
edition of *Écrits* from 1970, though he disputes the assertion that
he had, in fact, suggested that the dreamwork did think and claims
that the basis of his analysis is not delimited by linguistics. The
rupture that Lyotard assigns to desire as force is, however, clearly
different from that of Lacan. It is in this force of the figural to
disrupt – 'hand in glove with desire' – that Lyotard recognizes an

art that transgresses the here and now, and turns discourse into 'event', refusing to dissolve the energy of desire into language.[13]

Parts of *Discourse, Figure* had been worked out, 'week after week in front of us', through the course and seminar taught at Nanterre in 1967–8 and 1968–9.[14] Among those involved were Guy Fihman and Claudine Eizykman who, together with Lyotard and Dominique Avron, formed a workshop in experimental film that ran from 1967 to 1974, overlapping Lyotard's transfer to the new experimental university at Vincennes. Together they discussed both the functioning of desire in the cinematic image and engaged in making films, exploiting montage, superimposition and the new possibilities of video. One collaborative fifteen-minute film, *L'Autre scène*, critically explores an advert for Gillette – 'This blade loves your skin' – while a shorter 16 mm film-essay, credited only to Lyotard and titled *Mao Gillette*, continues to critique the conformity of both capitalist and Maoist image-making. Both films are preserved and made available for distribution by the Cinédoc Paris Films co-operative run by Eizykman and Fihman since 1974. An important archive of experimental film, it also preserves a video of the television programme *Tribune sans tribune* (1978), described at the opening of the present book; the control of the means of production, which was a prerequisite for his participation in the mainstream television broadcast, had clearly been informed by this practical experience. The activities of this workshop demonstrate another exploration of the interrelationship of theory and practice and helps us to understand the extent of Lyotard's practical experience – not expertise – in the area of visual arts. Consequently, he was at ease in sites of creative production, whether an artist's studio, arts faculty or art school.

Film and cinema were not, however, a major focus of his considerations – there is no equivalent to Deleuze's two-volume study of cinema, for example – and even though Monory and Gianfranco Baruchello, two of the artists about whom he wrote at length on several occasions, were also film-makers, Lyotard did not write about their films: 'I prefer his paintings to his films,' he said of Monory.[15] One essay on cinema that has made a recognized impact on film theory is 'Acinéma'. Published first in an edition of *Revue d'esthétique* devoted to cinema in 1973, on the condition that the other collaborators of *L'Autre scène* were also invited to contribute, it was subsequently reprinted in *Des dispositifs pulsionnels*. Whilst its celebration of experimental over mainstream cinema – because of its capacity to affect and distance audiences through extremes of movement, disorder and non-productive intensities, inducing the effect of *jouissance* – may seem to be bound up with specific debates of its time, there has been a reconsideration of Lyotard's contribution to film, resulting in three separate publications: in French (Durafour, 2009), Italian (Costa, ed., 2008) and English (Woodward and Jones, eds, 2017). It is perhaps because Lyotard does not present a theory, either for cinema or art more generally, that the field remains open for others to explore, responding to his prompts rather than suffocated by the constraints of a method. This openness to exploration can often be found in Lyotard's essays and interventions in the arts, such as his contribution in November 1976 to a conference at the University of Wisconsin, Milwaukee, organized by Michel Benamou under the title 'International Symposium on Post-modern Performance'.

The programme for the five-day event included contributions from several artists associated with Fluxus – John Cage, Allan Kaprow, Carolee Schneemann and Dick Higgins – a round table on Marcel Duchamp, in which Lyotard participated; a film screening; and poetry readings and lectures, including a contribution from Lyotard.[16] In this, titled 'The Unconscious as Mise-en-Scène', he reformulated one of the detailed discussions of a case study by Freud from *Discourse, Figure*, in relation to forms of staging presentation, including the film *La Région centrale* (1971) by Michael Snow. The device created for Snow's five days

Michael Snow with the machine used to film *La Région centrale* (1971) in October 1969.

of filming on top of an isolated rocky mountain top in northern Quebec allows the camera to turn 360° on multiple axes: filming land, sky and horizon from a multitude of angles, the film is at once both a demonstration and an illustration of the mechanism which produces it – a *dispositif* which elicits the reconfiguration of placings which are paralleled in Freud's case study 'A Child is Being Beaten'. Lyotard describes how the eponymous utterance of its title is reconfigured by the analysand and analyst in order to articulate the figural nature at work in the unconscious, driving the patient's responses – both bodily and linguistic – in a manner that recalls the camera-activating device which Snow designed with engineer Pierre Abeloos. The effect of watching *La Région centrale* is physically disorientating, accentuated by the soundtrack which recalls the electronic movements and pulses of the machine's remote-controlled dance – one that affects the viewer 'somatographically', transcribed onto the body.

The effects of Michael Snow's mechanized eye link not only to *Discourse, Figure* – 'This book is a defence of the eye' – but to the

Michael Snow, *La Région centrale* (1971), 16 mm film, colour, sound, 180 minutes, National Gallery of Canada, Ottawa.

device of the band and the bar in *Libidinal Economy* – 'a discourse of dissimulation'.[17] The turning, twisting bar of representation is a central figure which Lyotard attempts to keep moving throughout *Libidinal Economy*; when it is allowed to slow down, it begins to separate into oppositions – like the signifier and signified of Saussure and linguistics, the dialectical thinking of Hegel or the representational space of the theatre, where the stage is separated from the world, itself a metaphor for metaphysics. In order to avoid such coalescence into binary forms of thinking, to maintain difference not opposition, the movement of the bar must be accelerated to create the libidinal band. Following the shape of a Möbius strip – a band with a single twist which ensures that the outside surface will also become the inside – the libidinal band provides the book with its striking opening command:

> Open the so-called body and spread out all its surfaces: not only the skin with each of its folds, wrinkles, scars, with its great velvety planes, and contiguous to that, the scalp and its mane

of hair, the tender pubic fur, nipples, nails, hard transparent skin under the heel, the light frills of the eyelids, set with lashes – but open and spread, expose the labia majora, so also the labia minora with their blue network bathed in mucus, dilate the diaphragm of the anal sphincter, longitudinally cut and flatten out the black conduit of the rectum . . . take them apart and put them end to end with . . . the cavernous body of the penis, and extract the great muscles, the great dorsal nets, spread them out like smooth sleeping dolphins. Work as the sun does when you're sunbathing or taking grass.[18]

Neither inside nor out, neither male nor female, the libidinal body is a collection of parts which can attach at any point: not substitution nor transgression – which presumes bodily unity – but the polymorphous perversity of heterogeneity in which libidinal intensities run free from 'the representative chamber', and critique is abandoned.[19] If theory is immobile, then Lyotard does everything to challenge this immobility, mocking those who refuse to acknowledge the perpetual revolution set in motion by the events of '68. In the section 'The Desire named Marx', early and late Marx – the 'Old Prosecutor Marx' and the 'Little Girl Marx' – become figures of parody. Both are denying their desires: dreaming of reconciliation, they distance themselves from the energies of capitalism, creating barriers, more oppositions, whereas it is capitalism which makes any relation possible, 'the displacement of what was in place . . . money being able to justify anything', as recognized by Marx's assessment of prostitution as the 'specific expression of the general prostitution of labour'.[20] *Libidinal Economy*, having rejected critique, expresses through extremities of rhetoric the challenges which dissident thinkers – Georges Bataille, Pierre Klossowski, de Sade, Nietzsche 'the madman' – bring to the orthodoxies of economic and political thinking, epitomized by the inflexible adherence to Marxism as a quasi-religion based on lack, the opposition of absence to presence in Lacan and St Augustine's *City of God*.

To do justice to this book in such a whirlwind tour is not possible, and justice is the one issue on which it has been frequently attacked, not least in the series of dialogues between Lyotard and Jean-Loup Thébaud published in 1977 as *Au juste* and translated as *Just Gaming*. Thébaud complains, 'the form of writing did not allow for any negotiating'; Lyotard replies, 'I wonder if any book is ever negotiable, in any case. I think books produce effects.'[21] It was also attacked severally in a special Lyotard issue of the journal *L'Arc*, in 1976, in which the editors found adversaries on every side ready to respond – every side, that is, except for former comrades in Socialisme ou Barbarie, none of whom contributed: *Libidinal Economy* had shown that Lyotard's position was not open to dialogue in the language of Marxism. A work that remains too neglected, it asks questions through the economy of its writing and challenges the boundaries of genres: how are certain books allowed to behave? When is writing permitted to walk free from the scholastic reiteration of established positions? As Nietzsche wrote in *The Gay Science*, 'Our first question about the value of a book, a person, or a piece of music is: "Can they walk?" Even more, "Can they dance?"'[22]

In the reprisals and questioning which followed the events of 1968, Lyotard was seen by the old guard as synonymous with the March 22 Movement; the Union of Communist students at Nanterre circulated a four-page pamphlet, *Le Solo funèbre de J. F. Lyotard* (The Funereal Solo of J. F. Lyotard), which accused him of 'mystification' and betraying the class struggle, but they also unwittingly give a useful description of his approach: 'We shall see that even this constant displacement is the logic of Lyotard's enterprise'– a type of dance, one which he is often seen to have been dancing with Deleuze at this time.[23] They both began teaching at Vincennes in the academic year 1970–71 and were to remain there until 1987, the remainder of their academic careers

Lyotard at the conference *Nietzsche aujourd'hui?*, Cerisy-la-Salle, July 1972.

in France. Having been a member on the panel for Lyotard's Doctorat d'État, Deleuze then wrote a short but enthusiastic review of *Discourse, Figure*, referring to Lyotard's book as a 'Schizo-livre, which across its complex technique, achieves a great clarity'.[24] In this article, Deleuze shows no sign of the reservations expressed in *Anti-Oedipe* (Anti-Oedipus) – famously co-written with psychoanalyst Félix Guattari, it had just been published with much media attention – that Lyotard's transgressions do not go far enough, revealing a different attitude to transgression, which indicates future differences between these thinkers who are often brought together in a supposedly shared libidinal philosophy.

However, the proximity of their shared interests at this time was clearly evident at the conference on Nietzsche in the summer of 1972, as the publisher Christian Bourgois recalls: 'They arrived together and left together and had a very similar reading of Nietzsche.'[25] *Nietzsche aujourd'hui?* was the title of the ten-day gathering (*décade*) held at the Centre Culturel de Cerisy-la-Salle, an important centre for academic discussions in France since 1952.

In his contribution 'Notes on the Return and Kapital', Lyotard took up Nietzsche's challenge to read intensively, reading the death instinct beyond the structural limits of Freud to the excess of Nietzsche's repetition which asks for more pleasure, more dissolution: 'the metamorphosis of things into men, of men into things, of products into means of production.'[26] It is a symbiotic relationship developed in *Libidinal Economy* as the willing prostitution of the worker before the machine, a masochistic submission in which the body is transformed: 'Modernity as the deeply *affirmative* character of such a dissolution,' he reflected at Cerisy, one which is epitomized for Lyotard in both the deadpan monochromatic blue of Monory's hyperrealist paintings and the machinic constructions of Marcel Duchamp.[27]

6

'A Report on Knowledge'

The stylistic shock of *Libidinal Economy*, with its scathing humour and scandalous disregard for the norms of academic argument, contrasts markedly with the sombre, analytical tone of *Le Différend* (The Differend: Phrases in Dispute), published in 1983. There remains, however, a wry smile evident in the 'Reading Dossier' which prefaces *The Differend*: outlining the objectives and approach of the book, it includes a summary to enable the reader 'to "talk about the book" without having read it'.[1] Lyotard also indicates here that he had 'begun this work right after the publication of *Économie Libidinale*', which helps to contextualize the many 'minor' publications – some on artists, some collections of essays – which accompanied the preparations of what he termed his 'book of philosophy'.

As one commentator responded, if this was his 'book of philosophy', what were the others?[2] It is a question worth asking, not only because Lyotard also claimed to have written 'three "real" books' (meaning *Discourse, Figure*; *Libidinal Economy*; and *The Differend*) but because it questions the status of the publication for which he became best known: *La Condition postmoderne* (The Postmodern Condition: A Report on Knowledge), written in 1979.[3] Writing in 1996, Stuart Sim describes how *The Postmodern Condition* became 'one of those texts that takes on a life of its own and becomes a general cultural phenomenon'.[4] Consequently, there have been complaints that the overemphasis on this text has led to a misrepresentation of Lyotard's thought. The resulting, often overly simplistic, association with postmodernism certainly began to infuriate Lyotard, whose efforts to clarify his use of the term 'postmodern' led to an attempted replacement, speaking instead of 'rewriting modernity'. Nevertheless *The Postmodern Condition* has a double role in our story, both as an event with consequences in Lyotard's life – bringing a new level of international fame – and as a 'report on knowledge', which can be related directly to his experiences with educational institutions: the experimental centre at Vincennes, as well as universities outside France.

Perhaps the most often-quoted phrase from *The Postmodern Condition* is Lyotard's description of the postmodern as 'incredulity toward metanarratives'; the full sentence is slightly more tentative: 'Simplifying to the extreme, I define *postmodern* as incredulity toward metanarratives.'[5] The legitimization of knowledge once endowed by a belief in the so called *grands récits* ('grand narratives' or 'metanarratives') of emancipation in politics or speculative reason in philosophy, and indicative of an all-encompassing world view, has been shaken in the technologically advanced societies. Lyotard continues: 'This incredulity is undoubtedly a product of progress in the sciences: but that progress in turn presupposes it.'[6] Science relies on its own grand narrative, as a producer of verifiable truths, for the legitimacy of its own claims to knowledge – one that is increasingly linked to economic investment: 'No money, no proof.'[7] Such a claim to legitimacy is based on the criteria of 'performativity' – extracting the maximum output while minimizing the input – which had once received unquestioned validation through the consensual basis of a grand narrative. With the onset of doubt, provoked in part by the challenges to classical physics by quantum theory, comes the incredulity that Lyotard identified and a crisis of knowledge, which together constitute the postmodern condition. The competing claims to the legitimacy of knowledge are investigated more thoroughly in *The Differend*, although its field of consideration is

largely limited to philosophical and ethical problems. To consider
some of the literary and artistic engagements which accompanied
these philosophical ruminations in the 1970s, we will turn to
Lyotard's work with Jacques Monory and Marcel Duchamp.

Lyotard had numerous encounters with the work of both
artists – one living, one dead – which resulted in several
books. The first extensive essay on Monory, published in
1973, was paired with a later essay to form *The Assassination
of Experience by Painting, Monory* in 1984; in 1977 Lyotard and
Monory collaborated on the book *Récits tremblants* (Trembling
Narratives) and in the same year, Lyotard formed his essays
on Duchamp into *Les Transformateurs Duchamp* (Duchamp's
TRANS/formers). These were all published by Michel Delorme
at Galilée, a small publishing house and gallery with a particular
interest in the interrelation between art and philosophy.

In *Récits tremblants*, Lyotard and Monory responded to their
shared experience of America in a violently sexual traversal of the
Californian desert in book form – one whose territory is shaken
by the opening fault lines made manifest in Monory's divided
photographs, reproduced once in black and white and then
repeated below, tinted his trademark blue and cut into disassembled
jigsaw pieces. Still untranslated, its title *Récits tremblants* indicates
the earthquake at the heart of the story, a none-too-subtle reference
to its explicit sexual drive which explores the folds and surfaces of
the dry Californian desert in a narrative fiction which shakes with
frustrated desire. In each of the eight sections, Lyotard adopts a
different tone, explores another level of the narrative, as though
searching for the detail that is available only to the technologized
eye, mirroring a similar preoccupation elsewhere in Lyotard's
writings. Whether through Michael Snow's camera-apparatus
or the multiplicity of Duchamp's Bachelor Machines, the search
aims not to capture and control, but to sweep over the scene in 'a
blossoming out', as Lyotard writes in *Duchamp's TRANS/formers*:

there is a blossoming out, in full daylight, of this unconscious of cunning implied in the invention of mechanisms that modern and contemporary technical thinking has silenced in favour of dominating and possessing nature.[8]

Duchamp's last work, *Étant donnés*, was unveiled posthumously in 1969, as a permanent installation in the Philadelphia Museum of Art. As a result, the multiple perspectives and means of presentation characteristic of his work seemed to continue to proliferate in an endless 'blossoming out'. There was a desire in France, in the 1970s, to reclaim their émigré son, and Duchamp became a topic for discussion again. Once resented as bourgeois and politically conformist by some young artists because of his silence over the Vietnam War, Duchamp had been kicked downstairs (visually), in an eight-panel painting shown at the *Narrative Figuration* exhibition in 1965, the last panel of which had his coffin draped in the stars and stripes of the United States.[9] In fact, Duchamp died in France, was buried in Rouen Cemetery and in 1977 was the subject of the first exhibition at the newly completed Centre Georges Pompidou in Paris.

Lyotard contributed to the catalogue of the exhibition, curated by Jean Clair, and in the same year published *Les Transformateurs Duchamp*. A work of hinges and incongruities, investigations of mechanized bodies and representational systems, it is deliberately fragmentary; Duchamp's own comment, 'I was thinking of a book, but I didn't like that idea', is used by Lyotard as an epigraph. This reference to *The Green Box* (1934), which contains reproductions of Duchamp's notes and preparatory drawings for *The Large Glass* (1915–23) – both of which also carry the longer title *La Mariée mise à nu par ses célibataires, même* (The Bride Stripped Bare by Her Bachelors, Even) – was made visually explicit when a first English translation of Lyotard's book was produced as a specialist art edition by Lapiz Press, California,

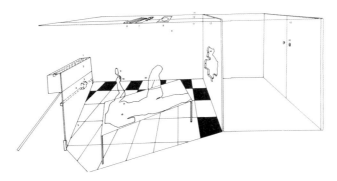

Line drawing by Lyotard, 'Approximate diagram of Étant donnés', published in Lyotard's *Les Transformateurs Duchamp*, 1977. © Editions Galilée.

in 1990. This edition encases Lyotard's text in blind-embossed green-flocked boards, similar to Duchamp's box. Deep within the pages of the book, images of *Étant donnés* fold out to allow the reader to see, first, the rough Spanish doors with two peepholes, and then the view through the holes: the body beyond – the diorama of a reclining nude, face hidden, legs open and arm outstretched to hold a gas light, with flickering waterfall beyond.

Duchamp's instructions and diagrams for the installation of the work are an important source for Lyotard; he was able to study them in Philadelphia thanks to the curator Anne d'Harnoncourt. The set-up is at once a construction and a revealing of the structured conventions of looking. The observer is challenged as to what he or she sees – the uncertain characteristics of the model's genitalia are revealed as the vanishing point of the installation. Lyotard notes that the denuded 'gaping orifice' is both a 'hole' and 'a vulva', while Amelia Jones points out there is no vulva, that Lyotard mistakenly refers to the labia majora and minora of which there is no evidence, only a 'shallow crevice with no exterior lips at all'.[10] The perspectival set-up refers back to Renaissance models, such as Leon Battista Alberti's *Costruzione legittima*, while directly referencing Albrecht Dürer's 1525 woodcut *Draftsman*

Albrecht Dürer, *Draftsman Making a Perspective Drawing of a Reclining Woman*, 1525, woodcut.

Making a Perspective Drawing of a Reclining Woman, in which the artist draws a reclining nude through a perspectival grid, his eyeline fixed between her legs; as Lynda Nead comments, 'the image recalls not simply the life class but also the gynaecological examination.'[11] In Duchamp's three-dimensional peep show, the visual confrontation not only exists between the eye of the viewer and the vulva of the model as vanishing point, but shows that these points are potentially reversible. The viewer and the viewed 'are symmetrical: if it is true that the latter is the vulva, then the vulva is the specular image of the voyeur-eyes; or, when these eyes think they see the vulva, they are seeing themselves. A cunt is he who sees', or in more idiomatic English, 'He who sees is a cunt' [*Con celui qui voit*].[12] So much for the mastering narrative of vision.

Unlike the lush Lapiz Press edition, the Galilée softback from 1977 has no green felt, but its typographic arrangement does emphasize the wordplay of its title: *Les Transformateurs Duchamp*. The field (*champ*) of transformation inherent both in Duchamp's name and that of his female alter ego, Rrose Sélavy (a homonym of *Eros, c'est la vie*), is present in Lyotard's opening 'declaration' on their 'contrariety' or 'incommensurability', and is visualized in the work illustrated on the cover: *Door: 11 rue Larrey* (1927).[13] A single door swings between two door frames, unable to close one space without opening another. This hinge between spaces, meanings and representations is in operation throughout Duchamp's work, and Lyotard's response, 'seeing is no more than saying', is a warning to the reader.[14] Duchamp's aphoristic sayings, 'his strange little jottings', attract Lyotard's eye: the 'sententious' sentences that accompany his visual work obscure and annoy the viewer. 'Do you know what purpose they have, what end they aim for?' asks Lyotard. His response reveals something of his own approach, not only to art and writing, but to philosophizing and teaching:

> Well, I don't see any except for one: to make us speak. To make us ask each other, or ourselves, about it. It leads us to make commentary on it. His highly obscure sentence calls for our sentences to comment sententiously on his sentence.[15]

More than two decades later, Lyotard, in his book on the Dutch painter Karel Appel, is still asking the same question. Initially published only in German, shortly before Lyotard's death in 1998, *Karel Appel: A Gesture of Colour* is a meditation on this question: what is it that drives us to respond to artworks, what is it to make commentary, particularly as a philosopher? Part of the answer is that it forces the philosopher to confront what he does not know: to be undone by the gesture. 'The artist called and calls to a philosopher, but one deprived, disarmed.'[16]

There is a connection here back to *The Postmodern Condition*, whose central theme is questioning the legitimacy of knowledge and contemplating the effects of its increased commodification. Lyotard declares himself 'a philosopher, not an expert. The latter knows what he knows and what he does not know: the former does not.'[17] Ostensibly a report on knowledge, as requested by the Council of Universities of the Government of Quebec, it has maintained an influence beyond its expected shelf life, in part because of its ability to reflect the developments being played out in education throughout the industrialized world.

Mass higher education is used by governments as a means to increase the economic value of its citizens, while global trade and migration ensure that manufactured commodities are available at a reduced price. The original report ends its introduction with a comment on the crisis of knowledge as exemplified by the status of the report itself, a report written by Lyotard 'on commission' for the Council of Universities, a consultative body for the Ministry of Education, whose task is to administer the institutions of knowledge. 'There is, in effect, a blind spot in Western knowledge; it knows many things, but not what it is.'[18]

The Postmodern Condition was written against the backdrop of change in Lyotard's home institution: the imminent move of the University of Paris VIII from Vincennes to St Denis was seen by many to conclude a gradual process of normalization of the original experimental university centre. Innovations in the philosophy department strove to avoid this, however, through the establishment of the Institut polytechnique de philosophie, to which Lyotard dedicates the report: 'at this very postmodern moment where this University risks disappearing and the Institute is just beginning'.[19]

The Experimental University Centre of Vincennes had been founded as a direct and rapid response to the events of May 1968, part of the reforms initiated by the Minister for Education, Edgar Faure. Occupying a site to the east of Paris in the forest of Vincennes and leased from the army for a period of ten years, its prefabricated buildings appeared quickly among the trees in the autumn of 1968. In January the following year, Vincennes received its first students; numbering some 5,000, the campus was already overcrowded. What set Vincennes apart was its promotion of interdisciplinarity, new subjects including film-making and psychoanalysis, and an acceptance of students who had not passed the baccalaureate, but who fulfilled more rudimentary requirements, thereby welcoming students direct from the workplace or those looking after children – a crèche and a nursery school opened on site. The department of philosophy was initially created by Michel Foucault, who had a free hand to appoint staff; he 'was determined to recruit the best members of the rising generation', and in so doing brought together figures with contrasting philosophical and political views, including the Maoist daughter of Lacan, Judith Miller, and her husband Jacques-Alain Miller.[20] Considering the political make-up of the department, Foucault's biographer David Macey relays suggestions that it either represented an attempt to create a political balance, or a space for those marginalized by their previous institutions: 'Whatever his precise motives, Foucault had succeeded in creating a political hornets' nest.'[21]

The consequences of this turbulent mix had already become manifest before Lyotard's arrival, resulting in the departure of Étienne Balibar – antagonized by the Maoist tendency for his links to Althusser and the Communist Party (PCF) – and the forced removal of Judith Miller, whose declared intention to ensure the university functioned 'worse and worse' (being an organ of the capitalist state) was unwittingly recorded, published and read by government officials.[22] Foucault's own departure was, on the contrary, to a more established institution – in fact the pinnacle of French academia – when he was elected to a chair at the Collège de France, an appointment for which Paul Ricoeur had also been considered. Foucault's departure left François Châtelet as head of department; he appointed Lyotard, and also Deleuze, who had been unable to take up an earlier appointment by Foucault because of ill health. Remarkably, this 'legitimate troika', as Alain Badiou was to name them, were all non-*normaliens*; the exception to this group, who steered the philosophy department across difficult terrain for more than a decade, was Réné Schérer, whose traditional route via the École Normale Supérieure was followed by an involvement with Guy Hocquenghem and the Homosexual Front for Revolutionary Action.[23] In spite of Judith

Miller's departure, Jacques-Alain Miller and the politically radical (Maoist) Alain Badiou continued to present difficulties to the operation of the department, the latter devising a course which required his students to conduct a political audit of the other courses being taught in the department. Badiou's band of students were known to disrupt classes frequently and intimidate both staff and other students. It is a situation for which Badiou later expressed regret, and in the 1980s, he and Lyotard were to have a productive exchange in response to *The Differend*. In the 1970s, however, Badiou describes the 'political gulf' which existed: 'Proving, in rigorous terms, that Maoism was a sham was one of the specialities of Lyotard and his friends.'[24] Lyotard was, understandably, hostile to interruptions by the Maoists and clearly objected to their unwavering ideological adherence. Pascal Auger, experimental film-maker and former student, recounts how during one intervention, Lyotard was taken by force into the next room, 'where he was submitted to a sort of interrogation, I later learned . . . while us good students waited for Lyotard to return.'[25]

Challenges also frequently presented themselves from outside Vincennes: a hostile press was keen to mock the radical pretentions of the new institution and inflame scandals with reports of drug-taking, vandalism and inadequate educational standards. Particularly difficult for the philosophy department was the decision taken by the Minister of Education, Olivier Guichard, to withdraw the right to confer nationally recognized degrees because of a perceived lack of breadth in the teaching of philosophy. The department dealt with this not insignificant obstacle by using it as an opportunity to question its role. In 1971 a proclamation to students by the teaching staff asked them to consider

HOW
– to be at university without dying of boredom
– to contribute freely and effectively to revolutionary

agitation, even if you are not a professional revolutionary
– to continue to benefit (?) from the 'advantages' of
the University anyhow (without hypocrisy).
That is not easy, if you are not content merely
to *survive* on the memories of May.[26]

It was also explained to students that as the experimental university centre became the University of Paris VIII in 1971, credits would be recognized if transferring to alternative institutions. For those remaining at Vincennes for higher study, doctorate-level awards were still available: for example, Lyotard and Deleuze jointly supervised the Doctorat d'État of Cyrille Martin (Kyril Ryjik), who, in 1973, defended his thesis 'Nietzsche and the Body of Caesar'.

In spite of these pressures, internal and external, the possibilities offered at Vincennes were welcomed by many students and staff. The lack of hierarchy and the mixture of students from different backgrounds contributed to a positive, refreshing approach, while the adoption of a system with major and minor elements encouraged the interweaving of disciplines. The seminars of Lyotard and Deleuze had gained a particular cachet in the mid-1970s, and it was necessary to arrive early to be sure of a seat, as many non-students also attended.[27] Courses were not tied to a particular level and in philosophy there was no progressive sequence of elements. As a result, explained Lyotard in an interview just prior to the move from Vincennes to Saint-Denis in 1980, it was necessary to experiment, 'if not permanently then frequently', in teaching and discussion, differentiating to allow for the various levels of knowledge and taking detours to explain through reference to other discipline areas. The floor was often given to students who would play a significant part in directing their studies, abandoning the 'control of knowledge' or the impression of philosophy as an isolated, unintelligible specialism.

Lyotard (left) and François Châtelet (right) at a general assembly of the 'Institut polytechnique de philosophie' at the University of Paris VIII, Vincennes, c. 1978.

> Often on a more or less naive question it turns out
> that it is essential to 'make a detour' by such a text of
> Spinoza, of Aristotle, of Joyce or of Eisenstein or to make
> a study of such and such logic or linguistic theory.[28]

There is an inclination to sensationalize Vincennes – yes, there were protests, disturbances, joints smoked in class, scandals – and yet 'the birds sang', recalls Pascal Auger somewhat wistfully, 'even the calamitous state of the buildings . . . gave the faculty part of its charm. And above all there was there the best French philosophy of the time.'[29]

A similar claim is also made by Dominique Grisoni, who collected and edited a volume in 1976 titled *Politiques de la philosophie*. Taking 1968 as his departure point, not for nostalgic reasons but as evidence of a 'rupture' with the conventional supports of philosophy, the five philosophers chosen – Châtelet, Derrida, Foucault, Lyotard and Serres – had become something else, Grisoni claims: 'an abstract and monstrous form, pompously baptized "Contemporary French Philosophy"', not a singular body, but one with many voices, and many entry points.[30] What is unusual in this assessment is that it comes from within France, not from North America, where such a body will later become baptized with another monstrous title – 'French Theory' – and whose diverse voices were often forced to make false harmonies.

Sometimes the monstrosity and dissonance of these French philosophers was heard in North America, before the false unity of 'French theory' was created. The *Schizo-Culture* conference, which took place in New York in November 1975, is perhaps the most infamous example of this clash of cultures. Organized by the newly formed Semiotext(e) collective and led by the French émigré Sylvère Lotringer, it was not an academic event. Despite Lotringer's position in the French department at Columbia University, Semiotext(e) was always held at arm's length. The long weekend event on 'Prisons and Madness' brought Foucault, Deleuze, Guattari and Lyotard together with figures from American countercultural and anti-psychiatry movements, including William Burroughs and R. D. Laing. Guattari was heckled by feminists, and Foucault was accused of being an agent of the CIA, while Hugh J. Silverman recalls that Lyotard 'gave a magnificent lecture criticizing "the Magisterial Discourse" – the University Master Lecture – and he did it with such mastery!'[31] Having been a student at Nanterre, Silverman was familiar with Lyotard's approach and could follow his delivery in French. The uninitiated anglophone audience was not so easily pleased, however, as the critic and philosopher Arthur C. Danto later relayed:

> Lyotard spoke in French, and there was a table with three people whose purpose was to translate what Lyotard was saying . . . and they couldn't agree![32]

This is the scenario used by Lotringer and Sande Cohen to introduce their account of *French Theory in America*, because it demonstrates the misinterpretation and misappropriation which would be typical of the uprooted, decontextualized ideas that crossed the Atlantic during the 1970s and 1980s. Danto, who shared a panel with Lyotard, was so bemused by the event – an 'event' is how Lotringer describes it – it is worth reading his report:

> Lyotard, a man who has what I think of as the *true gift of incoherence*. The rest of the French have been trying to achieve it, but he was born with it, like perfect pitch.[33]

Lyotard's provocation was not limited to his American audience: following his discourse on the sophists, the itinerant ancient Greek philosophers who accompanied many of his incursions into both his teaching and writings in the 1970s, Lyotard challenged Deleuze, Guattari and Foucault to respond to his attack on the master discourse. According to Lotringer, they refused to take up the challenge and left the room.[34] There were many intrusions, departures and frustrations during the weekend, and while Lotringer believed that the United States was more ready than France for the interventions of Deleuze, Guattari and Lyotard, it proved to be less easy to articulate to an audience who had not yet been exposed to their texts in translation. While Deleuze and Guattari stayed at the Chelsea Hotel with Jean-Jacques Lebel, the bilingual artist and organizer of happenings as a guide, Lyotard was hosted separately by the journal *Telos*. Although this political journal, founded by the Italian Paul Piccone, tended to publish writers associated with the Frankfurt School, at this time there were some on the editorial board with an interest in French thinkers, including John Fekete, Andrew Feenberg and Dick Howard. This was evidenced in articles and interviews with former Socialisme ou Barbarie members Lefort and Castoriadis, and, in February 1974, in the first article published in English by Lyotard, 'Adorno as the Devil'.

Lyotard's teaching visits were frequent, beginning in 1974 at the University of California, San Diego at the invitation of Fredric Jameson and Louis Marin, followed by engagements at several universities on both coasts. He then made transatlantic visits most years, as a visiting professor or invited speaker in the United States, Canada and Brazil. As was the case with most French philosophers visiting North America, it was departments other than philosophy who acted as host – most often departments of French or comparative literature, or research centres focusing on the humanities. Lyotard's writings which draw on these experiences most directly are those with a fictional drive: *Pacific Wall* and *Récits tremblants*. Both books suggest a sense of estrangement, not only that of the inevitable cultural and linguistic difference but a shift in status and specialism. In America, Lyotard was a philosopher without a home, a visiting professor called from the provinces to serve 'the empire' – a parallel with the wandering sophists.

The sophists are largely obscured from serious consideration in the history of philosophy, or presented only as figures of ridicule by the dominant voices of Classical philosophy – Plato and Aristotle – whose derisory use of the term 'sophistry' signifies the use of underhand, rhetorical devices and tricks, to win an argument through ruses rather than rigorous argument. But, claims Lyotard, it is these ruses which question accepted understandings of justice – when the weak argument is presented against the strong. 'On the Strength of the Weak' was the translated title of Lyotard's contribution to the *Schizo-Culture* conference in 1975; a significantly different version was included in the special issue of *L'Arc* in 1976, and the collection of 'pagan' writings *Rudiments païens* in 1977. Dominique Grisoni described the deformed body of 'Contemporary French Philosophy' as monstrous only if attempts are made to create a good form, to build a statue which prevents the multiple entrances and exits from opening, closing, collapsing and speaking. Because the body does speak: certainly the body of the 'inconsistent speakers', whose foreign accents 'fracture the Greek of their masters' and 'go as far as to make their bodies "speak" – for example, by farting'.[35] Such bodily interventions unsettle the respectable boundaries of those who believe they have a legitimate access to knowledge, to power: such 'bodies of weakness' can 'infiltrate the master discourse, laugh, and make one laugh'.[36] Such is the vulnerability of the teacher who has no set programme or syllabi to follow, who has to rely on his wits to convince the pupils to keep coming, in spite of the lack of official recognition at Vincennes. And yet they do keep coming, said a bemused Lyotard in 1978 – 'the rate of attendance in philosophy courses has, little by little, been on the rise' – while the lack of professional prestige means there is no temptation 'to say what should be thought', if you stay 'in your prefab bungalow in "the sticks"'.[37]

The withdrawal of official recognition should have put an end to the department of philosophy at Vincennes, but through the ruse devised at the end of the 1970s – named the Institut polytechnique de philosophie – Châtelet, Lyotard and Deleuze found a different way of giving legitimacy to the diplomas it awarded.[38] It was a temporary but necessary measure, which, through the suggestion that the written thesis be accompanied by a creative form – art work, film, score, set design – also gave recognition to alternative forms of knowledge, forms which escaped the maxim of 'performativity' endemic in the postmodern condition, showing that 'maximizing output' and 'minimizing input' with 'effective verification and good verdicts' could be resisted.[39]

7

Les Immatériaux

I am surrounded by wooden surfaces, a stylishly contemporary use of
the material which gives a warmth to the room. On one wall hangs a
portrait of Robert Desnos, on another a painting by Pierre Alechinsky;
behind me is the Panthéon, newly bright in its resurfaced facade.
Here, in the Bibliothèque littéraire Jacques Doucet, is the archive of
J.-F. Lyotard – a fitting location among the literary remains of the old
avant-garde: Stéphane Mallarmé, Robert Desnos, Pierre Klossowski,
but also André Malraux's papers, which Lyotard consulted while
preparing for *Signé Malraux* during the 1990s. Among other
documents, I have requested the soundtrack which accompanied
visitors to the giant exhibition *Les Immatériaux*, curated by Lyotard
and Thierry Chaput at the Pompidou Centre in 1985. Placed on my
desk is a cassette tape, a Memorex, with a handwritten card insert,
an outdated technology which has a 'retro' allure, not that of vinyl –
I have yet to hear anyone espouse the sound quality of a cassette tape –
but redolent of the melancholic materiality of obsolete technology, the
once new. Visitors to the exhibition had to wear radio headsets, the
latest prototype being developed by Philips, so that their experience
of the exhibition was not only visual but aural – that their senses
would be oriented and re-oriented while walking through the exhibits.
Les Immatériaux included exhibits whose diversity and complexity
make descriptions difficult, sending commentators back to the
allusions used in the press release and accompanying publications: a
labyrinth, a reduced monograph of the 'library of Babel' – as Lyotard

Poster for *Les Immatériaux*, 1985. Design by Luc Maillet/Grafibus.

described the exhibition in *Le Monde* – or 'The desert of reality itself' – as Jean Baudrillard was quoted on the soundtrack in a passage spliced with the famous cartographic fable of Jorge Luis Borges, 'On Exactitude in Science'.[1] One of the images sent out in the press pack shows the bombed-out shell of a stately home in Holland Park, London, where, among the rubble and charred rafters now open to the sky, several figures peruse the shelves of the library, transported from the scene of devastation. Such juxtapositions are present throughout *Les Immatériaux*, not only in the exhibits but in the varied responses of those who visited the fifth floor of the Pompidou Centre between 28 March and 15 July 1985.

With no facility to play the cassette tape presented to me at the Doucet, a literary library without a Sony Walkman, I went instead to the Bibliothèque Kandinsky at the Pompidou Centre: their copy was in the process of digitization and unavailable. Having not heard the soundtrack of *Les Immatériaux*, it has grown in significance for me in a manner that is typical, it seems, of the current resurgence of interest in the exhibition, particularly among those who did not experience it. The Swiss curator Hans Ulrich Obrist is one such enthusiast, who, explaining that he would not usually write about an exhibition he had not seen or experienced in person, makes an exception for *Les Immatériaux* 'because it is necessary to underline its importance in the history of curating, and indeed of art making.'[2] Obrist was enthused and intrigued by accounts of those who had experienced the bewildering array – or 'disarray' as Lyotard refers to it – of objects, sounds, smells and screens into which visitors were immersed at the Pompidou.[3] Referred to variously by Lyotard, Chaput and their team as a 'non-exhibition', a 'dramaturgy' and 'a work of art in itself', it is now acknowledged to have been an embryonic example of significant developments within exhibition and museum design, not least the rise of the curator as author, and consequently the adoption of exhibitions and expanded installation as an artistic practice used by artists.[4]

Banner for *Les Immatériaux* on the Centre Georges Pompidou, 1985.

30 Years after Les Immatériaux is a recent publication on the exhibition edited by Yuk Hui and Andreas Broeckmann; the latter spoke passionately at a conference in 2015 of the need to embark on extensive archival research and documentation 'before it is too late'.[5] Having encountered the chaos inside the three archive boxes, CCI 98–100, which store the images relating to the exhibition, I can share his frustration and admire Broeckmann's ambition to make a comprehensive approach to the archiving of this vast exhibition. Yet it is the gargantuan nature of the project itself which makes such a task necessarily unachievable: more than 200,000 visitors; more than fifty directly involved in the team; a similar number of industrial partners; academic partners; an accompanying series of musical performances organized by IRCAM (Institute for Research and Coordination in Acoustics/Music) – the experimental music unit based at the Pompidou; *Ciné immatériaux* – 45 evening screenings of film selections, coordinated by Claude Eizykman and Guy Fihman; a series of seminars with international speakers on architecture, science and philosophy; an accompanying exhibition on the voice in the public library also located in the Pompidou; five accompanying publications and additional guides, video documents and a specially commissioned film directed by Daniel Soutif and Paule Zajdermann. 'If we had a hundred years' . . . says Broeckmann.

Ironically, *Les Immatériaux* was also unusual in its process of self-archiving: part of the accompanying catalogue consists of sketches, plans, minutes of meetings, and internal and press communications leading up to the event. It was also the subject of two extensive visitor studies, one an ethnographic assessment by Nathalie Heinich, and another a statistical gathering of information via interactive computer terminals, part of the site named *Variables cachées* (Hidden Variables).[6] This excess of information is self-perpetuating, thanks to the efforts of those like Broeckmann and the digitization of archival documents at the Pompidou; it is also indicative of the philosophical problem on which Lyotard was commenting. The modernist desire to control everything, including information and materials, has not lessened as we shift from an anthropocentric Cartesian world view: we are at once both excited by the transformative potential of new technology and resistant to its potentially dehumanizing qualities. What *Les Immatériaux* aimed to question was the possibility of maintaining such a position of perceived mastery:

> to make the visitor realise how far this relationship is altered by the existence of 'new materials'. New materials, in a wide meaning of the term, are not merely materials which are new. They question the idea of Man as a being who works, who plans and who remembers: the idea of an author.[7]

Made to wear headsets, the visitors became isolated from one another, while immersed in a largely incomprehensible realm of spoken language – extracts of theory and literature from Beckett,

Exhibition view, *Les Immatériaux*, site: *conte et chanson modulaire*. Interactive 'audiovideotext' exhibit featuring a version of the ancient Egyptian statue *The Seated Scribe*.

Artaud and Kleist, to Virilio and Barthes – and music, including Berio, Jonathan Harvey and Mesías Maiguashca, correlated obliquely with the location of the viewer in the exhibition. The soundtrack was broadcast through a network of infrared signals to 31 different zones within the exhibition, meaning that as the viewer moved into a different zone, the soundtrack would change, although as the exhibition itself was divided into approximately sixty sites, this transition did not necessarily align clearly with the viewer's movement to a new site. Some visitors remained unaware that it was their position which altered the soundtrack; others resented being made to wear the headset, and the visitors' book records the frustration of guests who experienced malfunctioning equipment.[8]

Had I been able to listen to the cassette tape with which I was presented at the Bibliothèque Doucet, I would have heard the recordings in a fixed sequence, divorced from their spatially curated performance, separated from the dimly lit corridors of grey mesh and the theatrical lighting which created the labyrinthine *parcours* between holograms, videos and the latest technological innovations of the early 1980s: synthetic food, synthetic smells, synthetic skin – the new in biology, in microelectronics and in sculpture and painting (which were precisely not made of the expected media but rather of electrical media and neon by Takis and Joseph Kosuth, or were assemblages by earlier purveyors of the new like Raoul Hausmann's mechanical Dada head, *The Spirit of our Times*). Nevertheless, I could have tried to devise an imaginary route through the exhibition space, with the aid of the bewilderingly complex plan drawn up by the exhibition's architect Philippe Délis, reproduced in the exhibition's publications: entering through the specially built tunnel, I pick up my headphones and approach the ancient Egyptian bas-relief of Nectanebo II – the last pharaoh, receiving a sign of life from a goddess – imagining the sound of 'blood pumping' or 'breathing', described by reviewers in the dimly lit entrance way, before emerging to the 'Theatre of the Non-body'. Here is one space where the soundtrack and the exhibits do come together clearly: an extract from Beckett – 'I gave up before birth, it's not possible otherwise, but birth there had to be, it was he. I was inside' – played in front of five dioramas of stage sets designed by the Beckett scenographer Jean-Claude Fall.[9] Each diorama introduces a gateway to one of the five themes which structure the exhibition; each opens a meandering pathway across loosely connected sites, while tracing the questions aligned to a complex nesting of themes and questions relating to an adapted model of early communications theory.

A brief description of this nesting follows: a message is communicated in relation to five poles – sender, receiver, support, referent and code – of which Harold Lasswell asks, 'Who says what? To whom? Through what channel? To what effect?' This model is then adapted by Lyotard to question the identity of the author in the world of immaterials and to coincide with five variants on the theme of *Les Immatériaux*, each taken from a shared Indo-European root:

Exhibition view, *Les Immatériaux*, site: *arôme simulé*.

'*mât*: to make by hand, to measure, to build.'[10] Consequently, the themes chosen for the five wandering routes through the exhibition are made to correspond to the following questions: through what does it speak (*matériau*/medium)? In whose name does it speak (*maternité*/maternity, emitter of the message)? Of what does it speak (*matière*/matter, referent)? To what end does it speak (*matériel*/material, receiver)? In what does it speak (*matrice*/matrix, code)? Despite – or more precisely, because of – the complexity of this set-up, Lyotard maintains that the aim of the exhibition 'is a precise one: to arouse the visitor's reflection and his anxiety about the postmodern condition' by questioning the assumption of mastery implicit in the anthropocentric models of communication on which modern communication systems have been built.[11]

What is both interesting and difficult is the placing of *Les Immatériaux* within Lyotard's life and work. At the outset of this book, I highlighted the risk of attempting to present his work as a connected whole, and felt reassured only because I knew holes in the story would remain. Despite several breaks within Lyotard's life and work – whether personal, philosophical or political – connections do, of course, remain. Perhaps a useful illustration would be the set-up of *Les Immatériaux* as analogous to the ways in which his interests overlap: the zones of the soundtrack covered several sites at once but also, at times, fell silent – the areas he referred to as deserts. Similarly, *Les Immatériaux* can be seen to relate to several areas of Lyotard's thought, the most obvious being the postmodern, but it would be wrong to see it simply as an illustration, or even an enactment, of an existing text: rather it was a different way of thinking through a philosophical problem, worked through with a large team and presented to visitors not as a predetermined thesis, but as a series of questions to which they were called to respond.

The project which became *Les Immatériaux* had been in development by Thierry Chaput and his team at the Centre de création industrielle (the design and architecture centre at the Pompidou) for more than a year when Lyotard was approached in May 1983. Later that year, Lyotard signed a contract appointing him as Chief Curator, although Thierry Chaput was always considered the co-curator, and his initiatives are explicitly credited by Lyotard: whether to use the suspended metal mesh as the scenographic basis, or the concept of the *Épreuves d'écriture* (Writing Proofs), an important element of the exhibition's conception, which will be further detailed below. The developmental stages of the exhibition are carefully traced in a long article by Antony Hudek, whose exploration of the archive reveals the extent to which many of the 'innovative features that found their way into *Les Immatériaux*' were already in evidence before Lyotard's arrival.[12] In one of the publications produced in relation to the exhibition, Thierry Chaput recalls how their initial focus was on 'the challenge launched by technoscience to the old cultural matrix . . . Straight away the emphasis was put on notions such as destabilization, the uncertainty of concepts.' These were issues

Lyotard during the opening of *Les Immatériaux*, 26 March 1985 (from left to right: Claude Pompidou, Thierry Chaput, Lyotard, Jack Lang).

with which Lyotard had engaged in *The Postmodern Condition*; as a consequence, Chaput recounts, 'We had to call him . . .'[13] Aware of the risks of approaching a philosopher to become part of their project, Chaput describes the thrill of this radical venture. It was to be the first time a philosopher was so deeply involved in such a project – one which paved the way for future collaborations including Bernard Stiegler at the Pompidou's public library (1987) and, later, Derrida (1990) and Julia Kristeva (1998) at the Louvre.

Lyotard was called to the Pompidou because of *The Postmodern Condition*, the report which brought him fame on both sides of the Atlantic, and this connection remains clear in the opening to the press pack: 'The debate is open – it is international – on the question of the postmodern.'[14] The desire to have Lyotard on board was such that the exhibition schedule of the Pompidou's fifth floor was reorganized and the dates of the exhibition changed to accommodate Lyotard's existing commitments. Yet it has been curiously ignored by writers giving any sort of overview of Lyotard's work: there is nothing in the works by Geoffrey Bennington, Bill Readings, Gérald Sfez, Simon Malpas or Graham Jones; it is mentioned in passing by James Williams (in *Lyotard: Toward a Postmodern Philosophy*, 1998), and while the exhibition itself is the subject of dedicated books in Italian (Francesca Gallo, 2008) and German (Antonia Wunderlich, 2008) and an increasing number of articles, these tend to be in relation to exhibition history and media theory. Is there a fear or a reluctance to accept Lyotard's own challenge that philosophy needs to find alternative forms of 'inscription'?[15] Or does the sense of uncertainty which successfully filled the fifth floor of the Pompidou unsettle those more used to propositions fixed in print? Or is the perceived problem, rather, one of authorship?

Les Immatériaux was a collective endeavour, and the uneasy relationship of some elements within the exhibition are surely the result of this – Rolf Gehlhaar's popular interactive sound room ('Sound=Space') was, for example, perceived by him to be too successful and playfully out of keeping with the sombre nature of other exhibits – yet it is this uneasy coexistence which refused to make the exhibition a pedagogical experience.[16] In spite of the size of the challenge, the sense of a communal enterprise gave Lyotard a great personal excitement. Dolorès Lyotard, his second wife, describes the satisfaction that Jean-François found from working with a team, among young people, and while the ambition was certainly not matched by any practical experience on his part, his enthusiasm and generosity is commented on by other participants.[17] According to Hudek, *Les Immatériaux* offered an opportunity for Lyotard to reposition his contribution to the postmodern debate, one which had grown into an international phenomenon since the original publication of *La Condition postmoderne* in 1979 and whose confusion was exacerbated by the circumstances of its English translation in 1984. In contrast, *Le Différend* – published in 1983, the year Lyotard became involved in plans for the exhibition – makes no mention of the term 'postmodern'. *Le Différend* was not envisaged as a contribution to that debate: it was his 'book of philosophy' which staked out its terrain in relation to the philosophy of language, although its reception still dragged it back to the postmodern – in February 1984 a review in *Le Monde* was titled 'A Postmodern Philosophy'.[18]

Lyotard had spent the academic year 1981–2 writing *Le Différend*: officially seconded to The National Centre for Scientific Research (CNRS), he was effectively freed from teaching commitments at Paris VIII (which had just moved to its new site at Saint-Denis) and, similarly, there were no teaching visits to North America that year. The following year, Lyotard successfully applied to renew his secondment to CNRS for a second year, explaining that there had been a change of expectations, with the need to include and rework something of Kant's consideration of the historical-political problem on which he had just published in a collection directed by Jean-Luc Nancy and Lacoue-Labarthe.[19] The collection came from a research centre on the philosophy of the political, based at the ENS from 1980 to 1984, and included voices from differing political positions: Étienne Balibar's continued affiliation to Marx contrasted with the younger Luc Ferry, for example, although there was a shared disillusionment with the contemporary political situation. In 1981 France elected the first left-wing government, led by François Mitterrand, since the war; it succeeded only after much manoeuvring of the Socialist Party to accommodate and usurp support for the Communist Party (PCF). The PCF had seen its support decline in the previous decade, partly as a result of revelations from the Soviet Union, well illustrated by the publication of Alexander Solzhenitsyn's testimony and witness accounts of forced labour camps, *The Gulag Archipelago*, published in French in 1974.

Lyotard makes reference to Solzhenitsyn's account in 'Lessons in Paganism', first published as a short book in 1977, when he uses the phenomenon of the so-called 'Nouveaux Philosophes' (Bernard-Henri Lévy, André Glucksmann and others) to mock the shortcomings of the political system, and the reluctance of thinkers to follow the Marxist Left in the face of the collapse of its master-narrative. In this dialogue between differing voices, Lyotard creates a necessary distance between his own opposition to the PCF and that of the 'Nouveaux Philosophes' who had come to fame through their frequent presence in the media and a desire, somewhat opportunistic, to reject both Marx and the previous generation of thinkers, and to denounce revolutionary thought. Lyotard suggests that they had merely joined the dominant critique of Soviet Marxism in the wake of the 'narrative explosion' brought by Solzhenitsyn's accounts – the escape of thousands of little narratives 'which no one would listen to' before, 'when the Stalinist narrative reigned unchallenged'.[20]

It was a similar concern to provide a multiplicity of experiences in *Les Immatériaux*, without a didactic guiding narrative, that led Lyotard to focus on the pragmatics of communication – the internal interaction between the different poles identified in communication – and to pose the question of what might occur when these poles are neither human nor controlled by the human. Whatever the route taken through the sites of *Les Immatériaux*, the visitor emerged in the collection of zones named 'The Labyrinth of Language', where many screens presented opportunities for digital engagement: the chance to participate in an interactive novel or to access the results of *Épreuves d'écriture* (Writing Proofs) via one of five Minitel terminals (a telephone-based network which was the pride of French telecommunications at the time). Through a keyword or author search, the visitor could access the entries of 26 participants who had been invited by Lyotard and Chaput to accept an Olivetti M20 into their homes prior to the exhibition. Linked to a central server, these writers, philosophers, scientists and artists – including Derrida, Châtelet, Christine Buci-Glucksmann, Daniel

Exhibition view, *Les Immatériaux*, zone: *Labyrinthe du langage*.

Buren and Michel Butor – were asked to respond to fifty key words during two months in late 1984, not in order to arrive at a single dictionary definition but with the possibility of commenting on the modification and additions of other users: 'it was the differences which interested us the most.'[21] Of course, the form of this type of dialogue is now a quotidian reality, if not a banality, for many today, but the responses of those chosen to embrace this electronic writing machine in 1984 varied. Lyotard recalls that Butor took to it with ease, whereas Derrida referred to the machine as a 'monster', retreating to his own typewriter to complete his entries, which were then entered into the system by others.[22] Lyotard was so taken with what Derrida wrote that he later recompiled his entries – *Capture, Code, Confines, Corps, Désir* and others – and published them with his own response, 'Translator's Notes', in *Revue philosophique* in 1990.[23] In addition to being accessible in the exhibition and via any Minitel terminal for the duration of the exhibition, the results of *Épreuves d'écriture* also appeared in print form as one of the two volumes published in lieu of a traditional catalogue. Here the responses of the contributors – identified by a four-letter code corresponding to the first four letters of their surnames – are inserted under the different terms, arranged alphabetically, against the date and chronological order of their entries and cross-referenced with subsequent responses. Also included is an appendix of contributions which were delivered by hand when the technology refused to function, yet Lyotard was proud of its unusual form:

> It is probably a 'book' that elicits a kind of beauty, as it were, very different from what I was accustomed to. For me it is a great book.[24]

The accompanying volume 'Album et Inventaire' was similarly unconventional. Presented in a sealed silver package – as used for instant mashed potatoes – its two parts are held within a folder: in one side, a bound archive of the exhibition's preparatory notes and drawings, and on the other, 71 loose-leaf cards which correspond to the different sites, detailing the exhibits and the teams involved, many with additional notes by Lyotard. This frustratingly impractical solution to the curators' desire to maintain an aleatory element to all aspects of the visitor's experience is one of several Duchampian references incorporated into *Les Immatériaux* and whose endless games it echoes.

In *The Postmodern Condition* Lyotard had referred to the language games of Ludwig Wittgenstein, which emphasize the extent to which meaning remains in play without definitive rules for usage while organized according to particular self-legitimating types of utterances: 'every utterance should be thought of as a "move" in a game.'[25] In *The Differend*, the phrase 'language game' was rejected as implying too much control on the part of the player, replacing the anthropocentric connotations of this terminology with that of 'phrase regimens', according to which an utterance or gesture (a phrase) is situated: 'A phrase "happens". How can it be linked onto?'[26] The role of the visitor in *Les Immatériaux* was not simply to be a player in a game but to be asked how to

'Album et inventaire' catalogue for *Les Immatériaux* (left) and in its foil packaging. Design by Luc Maillet/Grafibus.

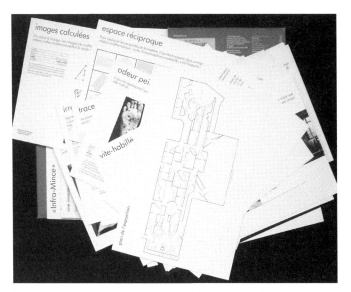

'Inventaire' part of the catalogue for *Les Immatériaux*, showing unbound sheets.

link onto the phrases presented: 'an investigator . . . accosted by the voices and the music, as well as by the sites he sees'.[27]

HEIN: About the exhibition itself, the main conclusion of my survey was the dramatic variety and instability of perceptions and reactions, from one visitor to another and even, sometimes, from one moment to another for the same visitor. (I found that the same phenomenon appeared in the journalists' reviews of the exhibition published in newspapers). This was not only the result of the misunderstandings I evoke above: it was mainly the result of a 'border effect', a consequence of innovation. The difficulty to formulate a firm opinion, to know 'what one should think about it', is particularly pronounced in front of something new.[28]

HUDE: The public's hostility – perfectly understandable given the absolute novelty of Lyotard's exhibition – compounded by Lyotard's own progressive disavowal of the 'postmodern' in his writing, has contributed over time to the elision of *Les Immatériaux* from most accounts of his oeuvre. I would argue that, far from being merely an aside, *Les Immatériaux* is essential not only to Lyotard's philosophy but also, *in its very elision*, to the constitution of a Lyotardian archive.[29]

LYOT: I keep telling myself, in fact, that the entirety of the exhibition could be thought of as a sign that refers to a missing signified. And this missing signified is what I was just explaining, in the sense that it's a question of the chagrin that surrounds the end of the modern age as well as the feeling of jubilation that's connected with the appearance of something new. But it's also, perhaps, a question of trying to underline something that concerns the identity of what we are and of the objects that surround us as it comes to expression through the material or through the immaterial.[30]

8

'A Blind Spot'

Lyotard refuses to show his face. '*M. J.-F. Lyotard refuse que l'on reproduise son visage.*' A blank page except for this short text, in lieu of the full-page portraits which accompany the other interviews in the second issue of *VH 101* – 'La Théorie' – Summer 1970. It is not made clear why this decision is taken, but it contrasts with the other twelve interviewees approached by Brigitte Devismes, the art magazine's editor, whose portraits are presented: Claude-Lévi Strauss pointing to a map of South America; Lucien Goldmann with his white cat staring at the camera; Roland Barthes captured mid-speech. It is not that Lyotard had a fear of the camera – that is clear from the images included in this book – but he refuses to accept unquestioned conventions of presentation, as indicated in his response to the interviewer's first question, concerning the role of theoretical research today. Lyotard replies that what is interesting is not to have a political theory but perhaps to take inspiration from

> what is happening in the 'arts' . . . to call in question and overturn [*de retourner*] a reality, social relationships, the relationships of men with things and other men, which are clearly intolerable. And, for me, that is the political dimension.[1]

Perhaps, retrospectively, we can also see in this refusal an objection to the role assigned to the 'intellectual' in French society. Lyotard was

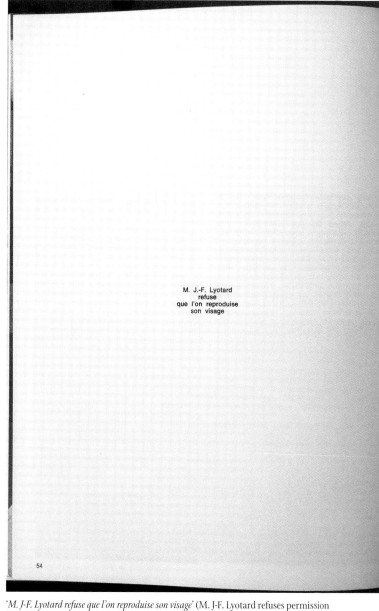

M. J.-F. Lyotard
refuse
que l'on reproduise
son visage

'*M. J-F. Lyotard refuse que l'on reproduise son visage*' (M. J-F. Lyotard refuses permission for his image to be reproduced), to accompany the interview with Lyotard in the magazine *VH 101*, summer 1970.

outspoken on this issue in 1983 when Max Gallo, the spokesperson of Mitterrand's government writing in *Le Monde*, bemoaned the lack of enthusiasm for the Socialist government among left-wing intellectuals – 'the silence of the intellectuals', Gallo had named it.[2] The title of Lyotard's response plays on this silence: 'Tomb of the Intellectual'.[3] Questioning what Gallo expects from 'the intellectuals', Lyotard takes issue not only with Gallo's misunderstanding – it is experts, technical 'ideas people' which Gallo wants, versed in the performativity of systems management – but with the French convention of the intellectuals as a class who wield an authority which extends beyond their specialism. Be it Sartre, Voltaire or Émile Zola, these intellectuals appeared to speak on behalf of a universal human subject. This is an obsolete artifice, Lyotard argues, which belongs to another age: 'there is no universal subject-victim.'[4]

Sartre had died in 1980, and with him the pretence that one can make judgements on behalf of a universal ideal. In an article published in *Critique* in February 1983, Lyotard called Sartre an intellectual with a 'vocation': a 'responsibility for curing the world of alienation'. Coming from Lyotard, this is not praise, but a damning indictment of a position of political certitude, 'I did not like the air of *capability* his writings exuded,' he writes, explaining that this confidence was built up to keep out earlier doubts concerning 'the redemptive role he had accorded the writer'.[5] Doubting authority, mocking authority, is perhaps Lyotard's one constant. This is not to suggest that Lyotard neglects political responsibility; it remains an ethical obligation, but one that takes a different form: a rigorous responsibility that insists on a rethinking of its position at every turn, unable to fall back on established criteria for judgement.

The question of judgement is a central and recurrent aspect of Lyotard's work; whether indeterminate judgement – not knowing how to act until the moment of the act, coming from a reading of Kant's *Critique of Judgement* – or the obligation of Jewish law

– accepting the call of the Other, without condition, informed by Levinas' philosophy of ethics. These are both addressed in *The Differend* but also continue to underpin much of Lyotard's work after its publication in 1983. While *Les Immatériaux* was open to the public, for example, Lyotard was teaching a course at Paris VIII (Saint-Denis) on 'Questions of the Sublime'. The Brazilian artist Patricia Azevedo, who was a student of philosophy at Saint-Denis at this time, describes Lyotard's teachings as precise and scientific, in contrast to those of Deleuze, who made a *dérive* through aspects of Spinoza over the course of the same academic year. Lyotard was able to tell the class what would be covered in the next session, and the course ended with a three-hour exam.[6] This precision is evident in the close reading of a section of Kant's *Critique of Judgement*, which was published as *Leçons sur l'analytique du sublime* (Lessons on the Analytic of the Sublime) in 1991. Lyotard's introductory notice explains, 'This is not a book but a collection of lessons' dedicated to the students 'who for years have endured its workings and reworking'.[7] What is particularly helpful in this text is Lyotard's account of Kant's approach, that which he terms a '"manner" (rather than a method)' employed in the Analytic of Aesthetic Judgement, one that Lyotard takes to be a guide to approaching philosophy in general and which borrows its reflective judgement from fine art:

> Thought must 'linger', must suspend its adherence to what it thinks it knows. It must remain open to what will orientate its critical examination: a feeling. The critique must inquire into the 'dwelling place' of a judgement's legitimation.[8]

This quotation highlights the importance of 'feeling' (*sentiment*), which plays a recurrent role in *The Differend* as that which signals what cannot be phrased, yet which demands to be linked onto, highlighting a differend.

The format of *The Differend* is sparse and precise, the result of much paring down to keep it short and focused. Consequently, it takes the form of a series of numbered paragraphs, interspersed with more detailed 'notices': on the sophists – Protagoras, Gorgias and Antisthenes; philosophers – Plato, Aristotle, Hegel, Levinas and Kant; people and events – Gertrude Stein, the Cashinahua Indians of South America and the Declaration of 1789. Left to stand without footnotes, its form acknowledges a debt to Wittgenstein – both *Philosophical Investigations* and *Zettel*, the collection of fragments and notes left in a box file at the time of Wittgenstein's death. What late Wittgenstein and Lyotard share in this mode of writing is a refusal to create, or attempt to create, a 'total' philosophy. Lyotard describes how the 'order' of *The Differend* is 'more that of an unfinished reflection; it is reflexive-argumentative, but inconclusive [*in-conclu*]'.[9] This resistance to any concluding phrase – a phrase which presumes to conclude – and the rejection of predetermined rules for judgement is what Lyotard takes from Kant: reflexive judgement not only as the criteria for the aesthetic, but for the political. The intensity of discussions and arguments, fuelled by necessary disagreements, is something which David Carroll remembers of the time he shared with Lyotard at the University of California, Irvine:

> I gradually began to understand that this was because to recognize and eventually discuss irresolvable disagreement, the différends both separating and linking us, was in fact the real point of the discussions, the reason for continuing to discuss – and to disagree.[10]

Throughout the 1980s, Lyotard's writings developed through an engagement with the work of others dealing with similar questions relating to justice, the political and the legacy of phenomenology, especially that of Heidegger. There were also international debates, provoked for the most part by a narrow reading of *The Postmodern Condition*, to which Lyotard was surprisingly ready to be drawn. For example, Lacoue-Labarthe asked Lyotard why he was willing to negotiate with the German philosopher Jürgen Habermas, who had called Lyotard 'a neo-conservative': 'why take seriously a kind of dinosaur from the *Aufklärung*? [Enlightenment] And why go after him?'[11] Other German philosophers entered the debate, such as Manfred Frank who wrote an imagined mediation between the two in print. In Frank's book, the emancipation narrative of Habermas, which relied on reaching a 'communicative' consensus, is pitted against the dissensus of Lyotard's differend, which explicitly denounced attempts at continuing such grand narratives.[12] Frank's argument is an extensive consideration of the different ways in which the two thinkers read important works of, predominantly, German philosophy. This Franco-Germanic cultural exchange presents an important frame for the discussions taking place against the backdrop of the wider 'postmodern' debate.

The reception of Lyotard's thought in Germany has a particular history, of which the encounter with Habermas (which never took place as a live event) is only part of the story. Lyotard's work begins to appear in German translation from 1977 and in 1985 *Immaterialität und Postmoderne* brings a discussion of *Les Immatériaux* into close proximity to ideas from *The Postmodern Condition* and *The Differend* through a collection of articles and interviews, including one with Bernard Blistène, which has only recently been published in French, and an interview with Derrida, which is yet to appear in English. German translations of *The Differend* and the collection *The Inhuman* appeared in 1989, but it was the publication of *Heidegger and 'the jews'* in 1988, in both French and German, which focused attention on the debates which had hitherto been largely a 'French affair'. Lyotard deliberately constructs 'the jews' as a term – using lower case and inverted commas – to indicate what it does not seek to represent: neither a nation nor a subject, but rather an issue of forgetting. That which Western thought forgets: an unpresentable debt. In January 1989, addressing packed halls in Vienna and Freiburg, Lyotard explained his involvement in the debate:

> I wanted to intervene to try to understand Heidegger's silence on the subject of the *Shoah*, to which Adorno had given the generic title of 'Auschwitz'.[13]

Lyotard suggests that the publication, in 1987, of Farías's collection of documents on Heidegger's complicity with the Nazi party had provoked such a debate in France because of their indebtedness to a German critical tradition; in post-war Germany, philosophers had turned instead to the linguistic rationalism of the Anglo-American tradition, of dialogue and consensus. In this conference, Lyotard specifies that the politics of Heidegger presents a problem to the French because it means that 'the task of rewriting and deconstruction that they have undertaken along with Heidegger is not innocent of the worst kind of erring'.[14] What might appear here to be a polemic against deconstruction is played out in *Heidegger and 'the jews'* with more complexity and complicity on the part of Lyotard, who adopts aspects of deconstruction in his analysis and accounts of Heidegger, Derrida and Lacoue-Labarthe. In spite of the, at times, virulent attacks on Heidegger's politics and his silence regarding his complicity with the National Socialist dictatorship, Lyotard accepts the importance of his philosophy – 'equal to the "greatest" thought'– but questions the positions taken by those French philosophers who have drawn on his work most closely.[15] Throughout the 1980s, Lyotard had benefited from a growing friendship with Derrida and discussions with thinkers close to him. This began with two important encounters at Cerisy in 1980 and 1982; speaking at the latter, Derrida suggested that in the story of 'Lyotard-et-moi', there would be, at the least, chapters named 'Husserl', 'Levinas' and 'Cerisy'.[16]

In 1980 Nancy and Lacoue-Labarthe organized the first Cerisy conference dedicated to the work of Derrida. It was titled *Les Fins de l'homme* (The Ends of Man) in reference to an eponymous lecture delivered in New York in 1968, in which Derrida had read Heidegger's 'Letter on Humanism' as a means of considering the contemporary state of philosophy in France. Derrida famously ended his lecture on the 'two ends of man', a Nietzschean double in which the anti-humanist 'over man' is inseparable from the humanist 'superior man', finally asking, 'But who, we?'[17] The presence of Lyotard at Cerisy in 1980 was of great symbolic significance because Derrida and Lyotard's previous encounter there in 1972 had been openly antagonistic. The *Nietzsche aujourd'hui?* conference had been marked by divisions with separate camps aligned to Deleuze, including Lyotard, and Derrida, including Nancy and Lacoue-Labarthe. Derrida recalls meeting Lyotard as he was preparing to speak: 'I'm sharpening my weapons', he had explained with a smile.[18] Derrida had left the conference early, before Lyotard embarked on an 'anti-Derridean outburst' which Lacoue-Labarthe later reported to him, yet the experience of the conference had left Derrida feeling isolated.[19] At this time, Derrida's philosophy was more readily received in the United States and it was here, a few years later, that Lyotard was seen to be making a deliberate effort to effect a personal reconciliation with Derrida while they were both teaching at Johns Hopkins University.[20]

In the intervening years between 1972 and 1980, Lyotard had withdrawn philosophically from the Deleuzian 'camp', and while they remained close as colleagues at Paris VIII, there had been a break of sorts. Perhaps the challenge thrown down at the *Schizo-Culture* conference of 1975 signalled the break, when he asserted that the externalized position of the 'schizo-culture trend' was 'exactly what the magisterial position and discourse asks for'.[21] Certainly Deleuze was to have no time for the postmodern, and even in a letter of friendship, written to Lyotard in the context of preparations for the special Lyotard edition of the journal *L'Arc* published in 1976, he questioned their philosophical proximity:

> One thing continues to surprise me, the more it happens that we have thoughts that are shared or similar, the more it happens that an irritating difference comes into sight which I don't even succeed in locating.[22]

Whatever the cause of this break, Deleuze remained one of the two most important contemporary philosophers for Lyotard; the other was Derrida.[23]

Derrida's presentation to the Cerisy conference in 1980 was titled 'Of an apocalyptic tone recently adopted in philosophy', in reference to a text by Kant. At the end of the ten days, Derrida felt the need to justify both his choice of title and to reflect on the increasing interest he had been taking in the work of Maurice Blanchot and Levinas in recent years, works which turned to religious themes, yet for which he could not share any expectation of the 'Other'. It was in this context that Lyotard presented *Discussions, ou: phraser 'après Auschwitz'* (Discussions, or Phrasing 'After Auschwitz'), aspects of which would become central to *The Differend*. It was not only Lyotard's approach which caused a stir, but his presence, as Avital Ronell explains, in 1989:

> No one was absolutely sure that he was going to be there when the time to honour Derrida came around. There had been so much silence between them, a break that no one really talks about . . . So Lyotard actually did come. It was maybe a kind of turning point.[24]

Lyotard's key reference is to Theodor Adorno's *Negative Dialectics,* whose final section opens with the subtitle 'After Auschwitz'. One of Lyotard's concerns is Adorno's periodizing of 'after' but also the naming of 'Auschwitz' and its consequences for Hegelian speculative reason: 'What would a result of "Auschwitz" consist in?' he asks.[25] While there was no repetition of the antagonistic scenes of 1972, Lyotard was not attending Cerisy to pay homage to Derrida but to question the residual Hegelianism in his thought and to raise Adorno's question, 'How do we "read the unreadable"', after 'Auschwitz'?[26] In doing so, Lyotard threw down a new challenge to Derrida: have we finished with judgement? We cannot finish with judgement, yet after the limit case that Adorno termed 'Auschwitz', we cannot approach judgement through Hegelian speculative dialectics, which always moves towards a positive result. This 'para-experience' cannot conform to the Hegelian example: it transforms speculative thought into that which Adorno termed 'negative dialectics', whereby all totalization, all homogenization and systematization is resisted.[27] We cannot finish with judgement; we make a judgement when we link onto a phrase – a phrase being some form of information, not necessarily linguistic: a gesture, a feeling or silence can be a phrase, for example – and even through our refusal to link, we have already done so, and silenced other possible linkages. A phrase exists; the question is, how is it linked, and in what idiom? How can 'Auschwitz' – Lyotard maintains quotation marks in order to problematize the naming of an event that exceeds the process of naming and to remind us of Adorno's usage as an indicator of a collective Idea – be linked, without reducing it to a subject of discourse within a universe of phrases, neutralizing its effect as an event that exceeds meaning and the system of communication that seeks to contain it? The argument is long and complex; it has itself become a focus for discussions in fields of study – Holocaust studies, trauma studies – which refuse to accept silence as a sign of forgetting, but see in it a sign that something remains to be phrased. When Lyotard was outlining his account of the universe of phrases for the first time at Cerisy, the implication was that there are linkages being made in Western thought which forget or silence the questions provoked by Adorno. Lyotard makes it clear at one point that he has not mentioned Heidegger, and in doing so opens a discussion which continues throughout the decade.

The title of the conference at Cerisy in 1982 was *Comment juger? À partir du travail de Jean-François Lyotard*. It attracted the participation of many who had been there two years previously and several directly took up the questions and challenges which Lyotard had presented. Derrida's response is described by Michèle Cohen-Halimi, whose book examines the relationship of Derrida and Lyotard through Adorno, as at once a response and a non-response: 'miming Lyotard's discourse in order to neutralize its tone and affect', Derrida draws on Lyotard's writings on Duchamp in order to explore their differences.[28] Cohen-Halimi suggests that Duchamp's mirrorical returns, hinges and the incompossible realities of *Door: 11 Rue Larrey* – the single door hinged between two openings – echo both the endless task of judgement and the extent to which the 'philosophical friendship' that links Lyotard and Derrida is 'not enough to make their thought indistinguishable'.[29] This proximity, yet difference, is commented on often: in 1980 Derrida spoke of his own propensity to nostalgia, in contrast to that of Lyotard, which he describes as having a 'tone of rupture with nostalgia'.[30] It is a comment Lyotard returns to later, in his commentary on Derrida's contribution to the *Les Immatériaux* writing experiment *Épreuves d'écriture*, and their differing associations with mourning become the dominant refrain – *Il n'y aura pas de deuil* [There shall be no mourning] – in Derrida's eulogy to Lyotard in 1999.[31] Through the intervening decades, we can, perhaps, see a shift of focus – away from the nostalgia of melancholia (which Freud terms the inability to move on from mourning) to a refusal of mourning itself. Derrida's characteristic wordplay, extensively evident in this beautiful homage to resistance, is not simply a stylistic device but a recognition of their shared task: to bear witness to that which cannot be presented, except through negation. As Lyotard had commented in 1980, at Cerisy,

> Adorno speaks of the legible, Derrida of the illegible. This is a radical divergence, and yet 'if *we* are the community of hostages of the "One who makes links", it is that we are learning to read, therefore that we do not know how to read, and that for *us*, to read is precisely to read the illegible.'[32]

The complex role of negation had long concerned Lyotard, as Derrida reminded his Cerisy audience: *Discourse, Figure* (1971) included a retranslation of Freud's text *Die Verneinung* (Negation) as an appendix. Lyotard argues that via negation, revealed through denial, the figural workings of desire in the unconscious are indicated: '. . . "It's *not* my mother" says the patient; "We amend this to: it is therefore his mother" says Freud.'[33] Freud's 'negation' (or more properly 'de-negation'), the Jewish law on the prohibition of sacred images, Kant's evocation of the sublime and the extermination of the Jews are all aspects of the 'unpresentable' which provoked Lyotard's engagements with aesthetics and politics.

In addition to the postmodern, Lyotard is perhaps still best known in English-speaking circles for his reconsideration of the sublime. As both these discussions have a tendency to overshadow his other work and fix it in a particular historical context of the 1980s, I am reluctant to reiterate these discussions here.[34] What is more helpful is to emphasize the extent to which Lyotard's consideration of the sublime took place as part of a wider turn in French philosophy to both Kant and ethical questions – as already indicated through the debates above – and to explore further his differing references to the 'unpresentable'. To begin, this term is in quotation marks because of its use by Kant in the *Critique of Judgement*, where he distinguishes between two forms of presentation and two forms of absence. The first form of presentation is a rational exposition through logical argument, focusing on the concept; the second concerns form, not concept, and is presented through an aesthetic mode (or 'manner'). Both also pertain to the 'unpresentable': Ideas of reason, such as 'liberty' or 'emancipation', are concepts which cannot be presented because they exceed the power of presentation. Ideas of imagination, however, are 'inscribed in the presentation' and consequently their mode of absence is related to the aesthetic manner: they cannot be presented as Ideas of reason, but they can be put forward negatively, without rational articulation, through the 'unpresentable'.[35] This brief summary comes from an account given by Lyotard in an extensive interview in 1987 which attempts to clarify the misunderstandings resulting from the use of the term 'unpresentable' in relation to his work. Of particular concern is a (still) widely disseminated essay printed in the U.S. art magazine *Artforum* with a misleading title: 'Presenting the unpresentable: the sublime'. It was included later in the collection *The Inhuman* with the corrected title 'Representation, Presentation, Unpresentable'.[36] In this and other essays, Lyotard exhorts artists to experiment, to question the presuppositions of their field and to turn to the aesthetic of the sublime because of its ability to attest to that which is unpresentable. It was written in 1982, and Lyotard still had Habermas in his sights. Contesting Habermas's claim that art should aid the building of a consensus, Lyotard argues that the experimental avant-garde which interest him 'do not call for the "common sense" of a shared pleasure':[37]

These works appear to the public of taste to be 'monsters', 'formless' objects, purely 'negative' entities (I'm deliberately using the terms Kant employs to characterize the occasions

that provoke the sublime sentiment). When the point
is to try to present that there is something that is not
presentable, you have to make presentation suffer.[38]

This makes Lyotard's approach to aesthetics, or that which David
Carroll appropriately termed 'paraesthetics', radically different
from many of the cultural manifestations of 'postmodernism' which
dominated aspects of art, architecture and design in the 1980s and
early 1990s, borrowing and reworking motifs and styles without,
necessarily, questioning existing modes of presentation.[39] And yet
there were sometimes connections, in the obsession with return
and reappropriation, with what Lyotard began to term 'rewriting
modernity', and the figure which characterized the role asked of art
and thought in *Heidegger and 'the jews'*: anamnesis.

What art can do is bear witness not to the sublime,
but to this aporia of art and to its pain. It does not say
the unsayable, but says that it cannot say it.[40]

The French edition of *Heidegger and 'the jews'* is dedicated
to Lyotard's father-in-law, the father of Andrée May, whose
deportation, return and death marked their family. It also
stands as part of Lyotard's long engagement with both German
philosophy and Jewish thought, one that has led to critical
debates even after his death, as illustrated by Elisabeth de
Fontenay's *Une tout autre histoire: Questions à Jean-François Lyotard*
(2006), in which her intense engagement with Lyotard's 'Jewish
questions' include disagreements but also a deep respect.

9

Childhood without Conclusion

Nul ne sait écrire. Lyotard opens *Lectures d'enfance* (1991) with this declaration of destitution:

Infans

Nobody knows how to write. Each one of us, the
'greatest' most of all, writes to capture via and in the
text something that we don't know how to write. Which
is not going to let itself be written, we know.

The narratives and essays that the present readings relate were
travelled along the trail of this poverty, this destitution. Like a
frontier, at once inside and outside, the line of disappointment
marks out an object for reflection, out there [*là-bas*], and
works over the text up close, at the level of its very writing.

The thing that these various writings hold in abeyance,
awaiting delivery, bears different names, names
of elision. Kafka calls it the indubitable, Sartre the
inarticulable, Joyce the inappropriable. For Freud it is
the infantile, for Valéry disorder, for Arendt, birth.

Let us baptise it *Infantia,* that which is not spoken [*qui ne se
parle pas*]. An infancy that is not an age and that does not pass,

with time. It haunts discourse and eludes it. Discourse never ceases trying to keep it at a distance, it is its separation. But it persists, by the same token, in constituting *enfance*, constituting it as lost. Unwittingly, discourse harbours *enfance* therefore. *Enfance* is its remnant. If *enfance* stays at home, it is not in spite of but because of the fact that it lodges with the adult.

Blanchot used to write: *Noli me legere*, you shall not read me. Whatever does not permit itself to be written, in writing, calls perhaps for a reader who no longer knows or does not yet know how to read: old people, children in school, drivelling, doting [radotant] over their open books.[1]

This translation of 'Infans' by Mary Lydon appears at the end of her article 'Veduta on *Discours, figure*', an account of the 'successive flashes of insight' that reward the reader of the 'notoriously difficult book' she was in the process of translating.[2] In *Discourse, Figure*, Lyotard traces a complex shift from the established schema of vision, to the unknown; he describes the elaborate image-making processes undertaken by Paul Klee to avoid formulaic approaches of vision – rotating, reversing, approaching from behind – and Paul Cézanne – wanting, willing to become one with Mount Sainte-Victoire. Lydon also highlights the slippage between the line and the letter that runs throughout *Discourse, Figure*, 'on the razor's edge between reading and seeing, seeing and saying', recalling that the same preoccupation traverses the essay written over a decade later on the drawings of Valerio Adami: *On dirait qu'une ligne . . .* ['It's as if a line . . .']³ It is one of Lyotard's most beautiful essays, and in Lydon's translation, her seductive rewriting allows the line of the text to invoke that missing element which called Lyotard to respond: a call coming from the drawings of Adami and to which Lydon, in turn, responds. Lyotard will later make the essay part of his book on the three artists Adami, Arakawa and Buren, who form his meditation on 'What to Paint?' (*Que Peindre?*): how do these artists approach the same question through their significantly different practices? Each time, Lyotard responds through a different cast of dialogic positions: Buren's analytical questioning of the framing of the art work, its 'institutional containers', provokes in Lyotard an exploration of the pragmatics at work in the artistic operation; the work of Arakawa, born in Japan and then living in the United States, is discussed in relation to his texts, to architectural collaboration and to thought and non-thought (the blank), through voices named 'East' and 'West'. But it is the figurative drawings and paintings of Adami that draw out a meditation on the line in the letter and the interrelationship of the two forms of inscription: artist and philosopher, each struggling to allow the one line to form at the expense of the others' potential.

When Lyotard sent proofs of the original French essay to Dolorès Rogozinski, in the spring of 1983, their relationship was in its infancy. They first met in 1980 at the Cerisy conference, she having recently moved to Paris from Lille with her husband, the philosopher Jacob Rogozinski. Dolorès was among those interested in Derrida and literature who returned to the Lyotard *décade* at Cerisy two years later. She has written of how, having resisted their love for more than a year, their affair began in January 1984.[4] Because of the strength of the bond between Andrée and Jean-François, Dolorès never imagined they could live together. They had a child, David, who was born in 1986 and, with Dolorès' husband's agreement, took the name Rogozinski. Despite attempts to keep the secret hidden, suspicions grew, and disclosure became unavoidable. The subsequent break and its consequences were profound for all involved, culminating in divorce in 1991. The biographical becomes, perhaps, a more integral part of 'late Lyotard', whether through the birth of his son – who could not take his name – or in the last unfinished writings on St Augustine's *Confessions*. But it is never just biographical, as Dolorès Lyotard writes:

It is always right to refuse positivism of biographical fact, to not lower the interpretation of the writing. But the point is, the literary person that I am thinks, like Stendhal, that the biographical cryptogram flags the virtual in creation.[5]

Here she is writing specifically about the secret codes included for her by Lyotard, in what he termed 'the perpetual letter', texts which include the experimental 'À l'écrit bâté', written in 1986.[6] Containing blocks of text, double justified and set without punctuation but with capital letters – though not where expected – it makes a demand of the reader, asks for patience and then refuses to cohere to an established form. The biographical layer helps but without reducing its possibilities, resonating as it does with the wider concerns of Lyotard's task to make writing sense without reducing it to the codified meanings of sense, to 'capture via and in the text something that we don't know how to write' as he wrote in 'Infans'.

The indeterminate, inconclusive story that weaves its way through 'À l'écrit bâté' evokes the interstitial space of the womb

Lyotard with David and Dolorès, December 1986.

where a child's future, its sex, its potential, exist in animated suspension. However, it is equally a text whose writing is deliberate in its illegitimacy: blind, it feels its way forward, unsure of its destination and equally unsure of its arrival. Odyssean in its wanderings and interwoven tales, as he writes of Joyce's *Ulysses* in *Lectures d'enfance*, 'How can one know that what returns is that which had disappeared?'[7] Elsewhere Lyotard writes of the infant as the 'inhuman' human. Born too early, it has yet to develop into a 'human': physically, linguistically, socially; and yet before it is born, it is already marked by the hopes, desires and expectations of its parents, of society. Already placed in a nexus of social nodes, it is thus named in advance, born into a strange inhuman relation to time.

The years surrounding David's birth were a difficult period for all concerned; Lyotard spent a lot of time away from France, with increasing commitments in the United States. In 1987 he retired from his post at Paris VIII and took up a visiting professorship at the University of California, Irvine, which he shared with Derrida and the Germanist Wolfgang Iser; each taught a different season: Lyotard, autumn; Iser, winter; and Derrida, spring. Although this meant that Lyotard and Derrida did not overlap physically, they occupied the same houses on Laguna Beach, and then Victoria Beach, and had both students and friends in common. Lyotard and Derrida's friendship had also grown through their involvement in shared projects, in particular the creation of the Collège international de philosophie in Paris. Derrida was integral to the creation of the Collège, which he termed an 'anti-institution'. Founded in 1982 to support philosophical research, free from the restraints and conventions which restricted conventional institutions, it was backed by the Mitterrand government as part of a programme to reinvigorate the importance of philosophy in French education. Lyotard's involvement had begun as a stand-in, during the illness of François Châtelet, but he was to take an important role in its development, conscious of the connection to Châtelet's model for the Institut polytechnique de philosophie established at Vincennes. With no fixed chairs, seminars open to all and at its centre a rolling programme of research projects and international visiting scholars, it represents the legacy of philosophical experimentation which once reigned at Vincennes. Officially founded in 1982 and open to scholars in 1984, it championed Derrida's desire for 'intersections' between philosophy and other areas of research; Derrida was the president for its first year, followed by Lyotard in 1985. Later, the Collège was to be an important location for Lyotard and Dolorès' work together in the 1990s.

At this time, many of Lyotard's previous Paris friendships had been significantly compromised by his separation from Andrée. Jean-François broke with the friends they shared and gave her his professor's pension and the family home. This apartment, at 62 rue Blomet in the fifteenth arrondissement, was close by his old school, the Lycée Buffon, and not far from his childhood home on the Boulevard de Vaugirard. Today, the nearby park, square de l'Oiseau Lunaire, 45–47 rue Blomet, is a reminder of the artists associated with Surrealism who lived, worked and visited studios on the site in the 1920s and '30s. These included André Masson, Joan Miró and Robert Desnos. In 1974 Miró's sculpture *Oiseau lunaire* was installed in the park in memory of Robert Desnos, who had been deported from Paris as a political prisoner in 1944 and died of typhoid in Theresienstadt concentration camp, one month after its liberation by Soviet forces. I have no anecdote about this park that relates directly to Lyotard, but its story seems to connect to the 'two sorts of inhuman' of which Lyotard writes, in a personal reflection that opens the collection of the same name, *L'Inhumain*:

It is indispensable to keep them dissociated. The inhumanity of the system which is currently being consolidated under the name of development (among others) must not be confused with the infinitely secret one of which the soul is hostage. To believe, as happened to me, that the first can take over from the second, give it expression, is a mistake. The system rather has the consequence of causing the forgetting of what escapes it. But the anguish is that of a mind haunted by a familiar and unknown guest which is agitating it, sending it delirious but also making it think – if one claims to exclude it, if one doesn't give it an outlet, one aggravates it. Discontent grows with this civilization, foreclosure along with information.[8]

This long quotation reflects well the inhuman that is also called *enfance*, while also highlighting the need to resist the acceleration that accompanies development, whether in the proliferation of new materials which mesmerized visitors to *Les Immatériaux*, or the energetics of desire that fuelled both capitalism and his libidinal writings. The reference to Freud (*Civilization and its Discontents*) is also an important indicator of a renewed engagement with psychoanalytic theory, one in which the emphasis on the force of desire which runs through *Discourse, Figure* and the libidinal writings is replaced by an attention to that which Freud termed the 'unconscious affect', and which Lacan, in his seminar of 1959–60, *The Ethics of Psychoanalysis*, first published in French in 1986, called 'the thing' (*la chose, das Ding*).

A reconsideration of earlier work appears in the section of *Que Peindre?* on Adami titled 'anamnesis': the character 'You' declares that 'I would not be able to work through the anamnesis of the visible without carrying out the anamnesis of *Discourse, Figure*', emphasizing that art is an ongoing work (art as labour), in the sense of obstetrics, as he later wrote of the artist and psychoanalyst Bracha Lichtenberg Ettinger, in an essay titled 'Anamnesis of the

Visible', presented in St Petersburg in 1993 and Jerusalem in 1995.[9] Lyotard draws a parallel between Freud's method of 'working through' (*Durcharbeitung*; *Perlaboration*) and Kant's reflective 'manner', discussed in *Lessons on the Analytic of the Sublime*, as a mode of 're-writing'. It is a 're-writing' that was also used in an attempt to approach modernity again, perhaps trying to approach the postmodern without calling its name, from behind, an attempt that is collected in *The Inhuman* as 'Rewriting Modernity'. Not unusually for the period, this essay also comes from a spoken presentation given outside France: of the sixteen papers collected in *The Inhuman*, seven originated in France, three in Germany, three in the United States, two in Italy and one in Belgium. Due to constraints of space, 'Italy' is a chapter of Lyotard's story which has not been given any attention in this book: neither the visits to the University of Urbino in the 1970s, nor the many Italian artists about whose work Lyotard wrote – Gianfranco Baruchello is a particularly unfortunate omission, so too Masaccio or Piero della Francesca. The latter's fresco *The Monterchi Madonna* is visited both in a meditation of the condition of love, in a short piece published in the weekly news magazine *Le Nouvel Observateur* in May 1985, and a decade later in the final chapter of *Signed, Malraux*. Here, it is the junior Malraux who discovers presence in the desire of the forbidden: '. . . come to me but death be to you if you desire me.'[10] As Dolorès notes, after Lyotard's death: 'For JFL, to "rewrite" meant passing from one state to another, the last almost foreign to the first.'[11]

'Rewriting Modernity' was delivered in the United States at the University of Wisconsin in 1986, only coming 'home' to French in 1988, included both in *L'Inhumain* and in a special issue of the *Cahiers de philosophie* titled 'Réécrire la modernité', which also includes interviews, a seminar discussion and responses to Lyotard's thought by the German thinkers Albrecht Wellmer and Manfred Frank. It might seem surprising to note that both Dolorès and Jacob Rogozinski contribute to this publication – both ask questions during a seminar discussion at the Pompidou in 1984, and in 1988 Jacob Rogozinski writes a response to Manfred Frank's imaginary Lyotard-Habermas dialogue – but relations between Lyotard and Jacob Rogozinski were comparatively unproblematic. From 1986 to 1992 Jacob Rogozinski took on the role of a programme director of the Collège international de philosophie and while his thought has maintained a closer connection to Derrida, rather than Lyotard, he has made provocative readings of *The Differend*, drawing attention to the role of Levinas in questioning the possibility of 'inscribing the ethical phrase through writing without doing it an injustice [*tort*]'.[12] The discussion of that which calls the writer to respond, central to the 'Levinas notice' of *The Differend*, is the question which recurs throughout Lyotard's later writings on art and literature, including *Signé Malraux*, *Chambre sourde* and *La Confession d'Augustin*

Although the title 'Rewriting Modernity' was the gift of the conference organizers in Wisconsin, it gave Lyotard the opportunity to consider the prefix 're-' and its implications for time, explaining that the process of rewriting is not remembering, not a re-inscription of the same whose future is a repetition of the past, but a listening to that which the past cannot say. The philosopher must listen, like the analyst, to the 'representatives without representation', signalled in the affect which indicates 'deferred action' – the *après-coup*, *Nachträglichkeit* – a surfacing of affect 'which appears paradoxical in regard to time'.[13] It forms the central focus of Lyotard's discussion of the Freudian case study 'Emma' – part of the uncompleted 'supplement to the Differend' published in *Misère de la philosophie* – and is integral to that which Lyotard terms 'anamnesis'. Affect is highlighted in the passage quoted from *The Inhuman* as that which escapes the system and is consequently forgotten by it, and variously named in the extract which opened this chapter as the 'indubitable', 'inarticulable', 'inappropriable'. That which Lyotard names 'anamnesis' seeks 'to recall what could not have been forgotten because it was not inscribed': never inscribed because, like trauma, the initial event escapes possible means of 'articulate' representation; yet its affect – its presence – remains.[14] Anamnesis is a working-through, as practised in the Freudian technique of 'free floating attention', paying equal attention to all elements, without mediation, without knowing what they are or where they might lead. This opening up is described similarly as a 'possibility', an active passivity, which draws on Levinas' unconditional openness to the Other and the heritage of Judaic thought, which 'represents a way of thinking entirely turned toward the incessant, interminable listening to and interpretation of a voice'.[15]

After their respective divorce proceedings, Jean-François and Dolorès settled in 'Fillerval', a country house north of Paris, while later also renting a small flat in the third arrondissement of Paris. Although a formal marriage arrangement had never been their intention, they married in 1993 at a small ceremony in the country to enable David to be officially recognized as their son and – with the agreement of Jacob Rogozinski – to take Lyotard's surname. *Audacieux* and *cavalier* are the words Dolorès frequently uses to describe his attitude, always expecting things to turn out all right, whereas the practicalities of motherhood and financial precariousness led Dolorès to take a more pragmatic approach. Perhaps the most significant evidence of this is the Malraux project, which was a joint endeavour: they needed money, biographies sell well in France compared to books of philosophy, and from these very practical concerns emerged one of the most surprising turns in Lyotard's late work. The fact that Dolorès is a literature specialist is also discernible in the interests which preoccupied Lyotard in this second part of his life: the preface to the *Lectures d'enfance* collection, included at the opening of this chapter, lists among its subjects Kafka, Joyce and Valéry, in addition to Freud, Sartre and Arendt. The literary is not a new exploration, however, but rather one which continues existing strands within his thought – most

Lyotard at home in 'Fillerval', Mouy, 1995.

evident in his writings on and with artists, including *Pacific Wall*, *Récits tremblants*, the writings on Jacques Monory and those on Adami adapted for *What to Paint?*. The Malraux project, however, gave him licence to push an aspect of his writing, previously found in the essay form, to the scale of a book: 'it's my novel' he claimed in a late interview.[16] Given the important intertwining of his teaching and thinking to the development of material for publication, Lyotard's working milieu is also an important factor, bound up at this time with the financial imperative to continue an academic career in the United States. One of his colleagues at Emory University in Atlanta was Philippe Bonnefis, Dolorès' doctoral supervisor from Lille, whose interest in figures such as Baudelaire, Céline and Pascal Quignard Lyotard shared, together with the 'estrangement' that literature can bring – whether in the challenge of Céline's antisemitism or writing's power to resist, not shedding light but writing 'against clarity . . . a bit of darkness cast over the lucid calculations of profitability'.[17] Lyotard's increased meditation on the literary, inasmuch as both the form and the subject of the later works pertain to the philosophical as intertwined with the artistic in written or visual form, was also helped by the fact that his experience in North America was within departments of French or comparative literature, where philosophical and literary concerns often came together. In contrast, the blurb on the French edition of *Signé Malraux* signals how much of a surprise the enterprise constituted in France:

> No one would have thought, before *Signé Malraux*, that Jean-François Lyotard, theoretician of 'la condition postmoderne', would one day be the archivist and explorer of the novelist of 'la Condition humaine'.[18]

In addition to his position at Irvine, Lyotard took up visiting professorships at Yale in 1991–2, and then Emory in 1992–4, before making Emory University his last academic home as the Robert W. Woodruff Professor of French and Philosophy. At the University of Paris VIII, Lyotard had been professor without chair from 1975 to 1987, never rising above '2ᵉ catégorie', while at Emory his prestigious chair carried the name of the philanthropist and former president of the Coca-Cola Company. While this initially seems an odd marker of cultural difference, the fact that Woodruff had himself left university without graduating – 'entering business before his formal graduation' – does mirror one aspect of the adventurer André Malraux, who became the only French Minister of Culture not to have passed the baccalaureate.[19] This is the audacity of Malraux that had appealed to Lyotard since he was a child and whose life he would make his own.

Having decided that a biography would make financial sense, Dolorès and Jean-François approached the publisher François George at Grasset together. Lyotard had the utopian notion that through their proximity, they might both write the book, bound together by that which Malraux named the *voix de gorge* (voice of the throat), the inner voice – as he writes in *La Condition humaine*, 'we hear our own voice through our throat and the voice of others through our ears.'[20] Striving to overcome such separation is the task of writing with intensity, Lyotard writes: 'Literature (like art) owes its sovereignty, as Bataille would later say, to its ability to share that which cannot be shared.'[21] Although the contract was signed 'by two hands', the practicalities of childcare, building a new home and the physical separation brought by Lyotard's engagements abroad meant that *Signé Malraux* is Jean-François' book to which Dolorès lent her ear. In the evenings, she would comment and mark the pages he had written; together they would discuss the approach taken, and later, when he became ill, she would check some of the details with Malraux's daughter, Florence Malraux.[22] But it was Jean-François' book. Dolorès also acted as a voice of resistance in the book's development: Lyotard proposed that the writing take a multivocal approach, similar to that which had been developed in *What to Paint?* and the essay 'Can Thought Go on Without a Body?' in *The Inhuman*. The latter is an extraordinary thought experiment acted out as a dialogue between two fictionalized positions – 'HE' and 'SHE' – in which 'SHE' argues that artificial intelligence can only begin to think if it experiences loss, suffering: 'Do you see what I mean? Otherwise why would they ever *start* thinking?'[23] But such a polyphony of voices, reminiscent of Diderot's *Rameau's Nephew*, would not satisfy the terms of the contract, she feared. 'Do you see what I mean?' He did not, and fumed at her opposition, but then, having reacted to the resistance, was to return with a subtle tapestry of voices and play of tenses which push and pull the reader in a web of association beyond the dramaturgy that was first proposed.

Lyotard's interest in Malraux is multifaceted: art, literature, myth, death, politics and a profound sense of sexual difference. He escapes the feminine childhood home, a smothering nest presided over by his mother 'Berthe, or the Spider', as the first chapter is titled, in search of the masculine virility he desired: forger, fighter, trickster. André's daughter Florence has it right, says Lyotard: '. . . he loved only one woman madly: de Gaulle.'[24] But the 24 years of service devoted to the General is not Lyotard's focus, contained as it is within the penultimate chapter – 'Witness' – although Lyotard does not overlook the minister's political complicity, his silence on the torture in Algeria or his hostility to Israel during the Six-Day War: 'Everything that revolts him, he now endorses.'[25] When Lyotard sent a copy of the finished book to his long-estranged comrade and founder of Socialisme ou Barbarie, Cornelius Castoriadis, the reply was one of thanks and surprise:

> . . . *pourquoi ce geste, après trente ans de <haine>*
> *pour ce <maquereau> (tes termes)?*

> [. . . why this gesture after thirty years of
> 'hate' for this 'pimp' (your terms)?].[26]

The 'witness' Malraux bore was to the contradictions of modernity, to the playing out of its grand narratives; but it is to the gesture of Malraux's writing that Lyotard responds, not the life of the individual. How could Lyotard coalesce a subject out of the fragments which Malraux himself created? How could Lyotard – for whom the dispossession of the subject is its constitution – write a biography, except as an illusion? The shifting ground on which Lyotard built his imagined biography – one whose thorough knowledge of Malraux's writings and extensive research are worn lightly – is the extraordinary storytelling within which Malraux enwrapped himself, the mythopoesis. Death and putrescence are found at every turn, as is the 'enigma' of sexual difference: 'did he do anything other than elaborate its enigma and its threat . . . ?', asks Lyotard.[27] This dread is personified by the earth that inhumes his baby brother – 'earthworms, ghastly larvae, arachnids' – in the remarkable opening scene, narrated by an eighteen-month-old Georges-André, for whom the affective response comes later, *après-coup*.[28]

Lyotard's small engagement diaries log the work's progress: March 1992, 'Fifteen Propositions for a Biography of Malraux', presented at Yale; 1993, eighty pages written and five interviews; August 1994, seventy pages and visits to the archive; June 1995 a dozen pages . . . There are other entries. But this gives an idea of the long duration of its labour.[29] In between are visits: to Italy, New York, Russia, Bogota, among many others; but he is 'always smiling', as he reminds his alter ego in 'Marie goes to Japan' (he also went to Tokyo twice, to speak of Arakawa and his 'beloved' Dôgen), which opens his collection *Postmodern Fables* of 1993. His leukaemia forced him to slow down, and the publication of *Signé Malraux* was put back twelve months – 'I'm not ill', he protested, but treatment and tiredness took over. It was published belatedly in September 1996, five years after the book was begun and two months before Malraux's ashes entered the Panthéon.

'You speak to a man on borrowed time,' he joked, darkly, in an interview in November 1996. It was an interview with the journalist Philippe Lançon, from *Libération*, which catches both his 'impish wit' and his enthusiasm and pessimism about human arrogance, including the stupidity of philosophers; yet, he reflects, 'it is exactly because we are so stupid that there is a witness to be brought.'[30] A witness to the gesture brought in writing, in art, in thought – that which drives the penitent Augustine to confess. 'To confess,' writes Lyotard, 'is to bring into language, to language what eludes language.'[31] In May and October 1997 Lyotard delivered two

André Malraux's ashes transferred to the Panthéon in Paris, 23 November 1996.

lectures at the Collège international de philosophie which became
the essay that forms part of *The Confession of Augustine*, but the
posthumous publication also includes working texts, fragments
and scattered elements. These fragmentary forms are suggestive
of future possibilities, anticipated in the opening of Lyotard's
second book on Malraux, the intimate *Chambre sourde* (Soundproof
Room), but only perhaps as a result of our inability to accept the
moment, which does not adhere to a succession of moments:

> There is no end without beginning. How could the end be
> known as end if it weren't recounted by someone? The narrative
> of the end of a certain time is told in a new time which retains
> that end – an end by which it presents itself as beginning. The
> relationship of our thought to succession prohibits it from
> immobilizing its movement on an instant without future.[32]

It is the instant, without future, that inhabits the inhuman of *enfance*: it does not know time – the affect that strikes before the means to inscribe it; 'It does not give testimony, it is the testimony.'[33] This is in contrast to the 'I' of the confessional self in Augustine's writing, which comes too early or arrives too late, 'postponing the instant of presence for all times', or the 'I' of Malraux in *Soundproof Room*: the figure of Lazarus, raised from the dead, on the threshold, which dominates Malraux's second volume of anti-memoirs, written in borrowed time after a serious illness in 1972, a few years before his death in 1976. The 'I-without-me' (*Je-sans-moi*) at the heart of Malraux's *Lazarus* is the intractable differend that separates the 'I' which writes from the Inner-human, the self, the ego, the inhuman, which does not know how to write – *Nul ne sait écrire* – yet which must.

On 21 April 1998, Jean-François Lyotard died from the leukaemia which had shadowed his last years and of which he was able to 'not know how to write'.

Without conclusion

So ends a short book, somewhat abruptly, after failed attempts to return to some of the themes with which it opened. It is not a circular life, neither one of linear progression. When some episodes seem to mirror others, they are accompanied by incongruities which deny the mirrored image – like trying to fit a right hand into a left-handed glove. In the essay *On dirait qu'une ligne*, Lyotard describes how the artist's task of responding to the call of the line is made possible only through the silencing of many others. In this book, some lines of Lyotard's life and work have been pursued, while others, inevitably, are left neglected. On occasion, it is the less familiar route, the way round the back, which has been taken: the unknown of Lyotard's childhood excursion, cycling with his sister to meet friends under the blue Vendée sky – 'the intensity of the first time; the authority of your life deferred, for one day . . .'[34]

The choices made may not live up to expectations, and inevitably some omissions will disappoint, but it is hoped that the reader will recognize the necessary hesitation – necessary because of a refusal to impose an easy coherence on either his life or his work.

To paraphrase Lyotard's approach voiced in a review of Deleuze and Guattari's *Anti-Oedipus*, 'Energumen Capitalism', we seek to provoke new shoots by branching off from the existing work, creating new spurts: flows or fugues. It is this capacity to invigorate new thought, new creative practice or new political reflection that makes Lyotard's life a critical one. Yes, it is difficult. Yes, it is demanding. Yes, it is breathtaking. But if we do not suffer from this challenge of thinking differently, why would we even start thinking? The suffering of the un-thought has many names: figural, childhood, inhuman, but also 'Algeria' – that which the system of global capitalism cannot accommodate, cannot inscribe except within its own terms of production. It is also that which he named 'the jews', the debt owed by Western thought which cannot be reconciled through a Hegelian *Aufhebung* (sublation). As Lyotard warned, 'This present "society" has no need for this affection nor for its preservation, it forecloses it more than any other.'[35] It is because he refuses to ignore this differend of affect that Lyotard continues to provoke, and continues to be political, throughout his writing.

At times he is outrageous – in his style, in his thought, in his refusal to accept unquestioned conventions – and this is mirrored in the multiple strands of his life, its many breaks and seeming non sequiturs, but also in the wry smile he gave as he sharpened his weapons. His refusal to play the game, or to accept the rules that are given, is never a pose. It is not a performance for the sake of effect, but enacted as a means to awake that which cannot be answered except by asking further questions and listening, always listening, to that which cannot be voiced: the interminable, intractable differend of thought.

References

Where published English translations exist, these are used as indicated; other translations are my own.

Introduction: Warning

1 Jean-François Lyotard, *Political Writings*, trans. Bill Readings and Kevin Paul Geiman (Minneapolis, MN, 1993), p. 90.
2 Ibid., pp. 91, 94. An evocative visual description of the programme is given in Tamara Chaplin, *Turning On the Mind: French Philosophers on Television* (Chicago, IL, 2007), pp. 167–73.
3 Kiff Bamford, *Lyotard and the 'figural' in Performance, Art and Writing* (London, 2012).
4 Hugh J. Silverman, ed., *Lyotard: Philosophy, Politics and the Sublime* (New York, 2002), p. 16.
5 Lyotard, *Political Writings*, p. 90.
6 Jean-François Lyotard, *The Lyotard Reader*, ed. Andrew Benjamin (Oxford, 1989), p. vi.
7 Jean-François Lyotard, *The Differend: Phrases in Dispute*, trans. Georges Van Den Abbeele (Manchester, 1988), p. 80.

1 Openings

1 Jean-François Lyotard and Annette Lévy-Willard, '"Entre apparence et absence": Le Philosophe Jean-François Lyotard est l'auteur d'un essai biographique de l'écrivain', *Libération* (23 November 1996), www.liberation.fr, accessed 16 October 2015.

2 Ibid.
3 Jean-François Lyotard, *Signed, Malraux*, trans. Robert Harvey (Minneapolis, MN, 1999), p. 80. Internal quotation from André Malraux, *Le Surnaturel*, vol. I (Paris, 1977), p. 7, emphasis by Lyotard.
4 Philippe Bonnefis, 'Passages of the Maya', in *Minima Memoria: Essays in the Wake of Jean-François Lyotard*, ed. Claire Nouvet, Zrinka Stahuljak and Kent Still (Stanford, CA, 2007), p. 171.
5 Lyotard, *Signed, Malraux*, p. 1.
6 J.-F. Lyotard, 'Foreword: Spaceship', in *Education and the Postmodern Condition*, trans. Rosemary Arnoux, ed. Michael Peters (London, 1995), p. xix.
7 Jean-François Lyotard, *Que Peindre? Adami, Arakawa, Buren/What to Paint? Adami, Arakawa, Buren*, trans. Antony Hudek (Leuven, 2012), p. 109.
8 Jean-François Lyotard, *The Postmodern Explained to Children: Correspondence 1982–1985*, trans. Julian Pefanis, Morgan Thomas et al. (London, 1992), p. 123.
9 Ibid., p. 22.
10 Alain Badiou links both their families' origins to Moudeyres, Haute-Loire (Auvergnes); see Alain Badiou, *Pocket Pantheon*, trans. David Macey (London and New York, 2009), p. 109.
11 Interview with Corinne Enaudeau and Laurence Kahn, 25 September 2015. I am indebted to Lyotard's daughters for their account of his early life; any related errors in the telling are my responsibility.
12 Badiou, *Pocket Pantheon*, p. 103.
13 Philippe Lançon, 'Jean-François Lyotard, 72 ans, moine-militant devenu philosophe a publié un (beau) livre sur Malraux', *Libération* (23 November 1996), www.liberation.fr, accessed 16 October 2015.
14 Ibid.
15 Jean-François Lyotard, *Political Writings*, trans. Bill Readings and Kevin Paul Geiman (Minneapolis, MN, 1993), p. 85.
16 Ibid., p. 135.
17 Jean-François Lyotard, *Peregrinations: Law, Form, Event* (New York, 1988), p. 4.
18 Ibid., pp. 5, 91.
19 Ibid., p. 17.
20 Ibid.

21 Philippe Lançon, 'Jean-François Lyotard'.

22 Richard Vinen, *The Unfree French: Life Under the Occupation* (New Haven, CT, 2006), pp. 140–41.

23 Pierre Gripari, 'Nés en 1925', *Les Temps modernes*, 32 (1948), pp. 2037–57.

24 Lyotard, *Political Writings*, p. 85.

25 Ibid., p. 86.

26 Ibid., p. 77.

27 André Chervel, 'Les Agrégés de l'enseignement secondaire. Répertoire 1809–1960', *Resources numeriques en histoire de l'éducation* (Digital Resources in the History of Education), www.rhe.ish-lyon.cnrs.fr, accessed 22 May 2016.

2 Politics

1 Jean-François Lyotard, *The Differend: Phrases in Dispute*, trans. Georges Van Den Abbeele (Manchester, 1988), p. 9.

2 Jean-François Lyotard, 'Decor' (1984), trans. Georges Van Den Abbeele, in *Jean-François Lyotard: Volume 1*, ed. Derek Robbins (London, 2004), p. 255. CRS – Compagnies Républicaines de Securité, a special police force under the jurisdiction of the minister of the interior. The reference is to the Algerian struggle for liberation.

3 Interview with Corinne Enaudeau and Laurence Kahn, 25 September 2015.

4 Andrée May, *L'Espace Marguerite: Empreintes d'enfance* (Paris, 1999), back cover.

5 Ibid., p. 26.

6 Mireille Calle, 'Entretien avec Jean-François Lyotard', in *Les Métamorphoses Butor* (Sainte-Foy, Québec, 1991), p. 61.

7 Jean-François Lyotard, *Political Writings*, trans. Bill Readings and Kevin Paul Geiman (Minneapolis, MN, 1993), p. 170.

8 Mohammed Ramdani, 'L'Algérie, un différend', in Jean-François Lyotard, *La Guerre des Algériens: Écrits, 1956–63* (Paris, 1989), p. 9.

9 Drawing on official national statistics, Kamel Kateb gives the figures for school attendance (ages 6–14) in 1954 as the following: for indigenous populations of Algeria 16.7 per cent of eligible children attended school, in contrast to 87.4% of eligible children from the

population of European heritage in Algeria. See Kamel Kateb, 'Les Séparations scolaires dans l'Algérie coloniale', *Insaniyat*, 25–6 (2004), pp. 65–100. See also Lyotard, *Political Writings*, p. 200.

10   The conflict was officially recognized as a war by France in 1999.

11   Soustelle quoted in Robert Gildea, *France Since 1945* (Oxford, 2002), p. 25.

12   Figures vary greatly: 'perhaps one million' is the account of James McMillan, *Twentieth-century France* (London and New York, 1991), p. 161; Todd Shepard, *The Invention of Decolonization: The Algerian War and the Remaking of France* (New York, 2006) cites French historians Sylvie Thénault and Raphaël Branche for the figure of at least 250,000 Algerians killed by French forces through summary executions, torture and population displacement (p. 9), but later (p. 10) notes Kamel Kateb's work which suggests a more likely figure would be 578,000.

13   Lyotard, *The Differend*, pp. 98–9.

14   Lyotard, *Political Writings*, p. 202.

15   Hélène Cixous, 'Bare Feet', in *An Algerian Childhood*, ed. Leila Sebbar, trans. Marjolijn Jager (St Paul, MN, 2001), pp. 55–63.

16   Benoît Peeters, *Derrida: A Biography*, trans. Andrew Brown (Cambridge, 2013), p. 21.

17   Jean-François Lyotard, *Peregrinations: Law, Form, Event* (New York, 1988), p. 66.

18   Lyotard, *Peregrinations*, pp. 64–5.

19   Ibid., p. 64.

20   Ibid., p. 65.

21   James Williams, *Lyotard and the Political* (London, 2000), pp. 9–13.

22   Ibid., p. 9.

23   Ibid., pp. 11–12.

24   Jean-François Lyotard, *Pérégrinations* (Paris, 1990), pp. 54–5. Lyotard made slight adaptations to this text when transcribing the French version from the earlier English version, hence the need to quote from the French here.

25   Lyotard, *Peregrinations: Law, Form, Event*, p. 26.

3 Algeria and After

1 Max Véga-Rittcr, 'Un An d'enseignement de la philosophie entre docte Sorbonne et ravin du Rhumel', *Les Bahuts du Rhumel*, 60 (May 2012), p. 4.

2 Pierre Merlin, 'Une Expérience dans la guerre d'Algérie', *Cahiers d'EMAM*, 23 (2014), pp. 61–5.

3 Stephen Hastings-King, *Looking for the proletariat: Socialisme ou Barbarie and the Problem of Worker Writing* (Chicago, IL, 2015), p. 246, n. 34.

4 Jean-François Lyotard, *Misère de la philosophie*, ed. Dolorès Lyotard (Paris, 2000), p. 177.

5 Jean-François Lyotard, *Phenomenology*, trans. Brian Beakley (New York, 1991), p. 51, n. 2.

6 Jean-François Lyotard, *Political Writings*, trans. Bill Readings and Kevin Paul Geiman (Minneapolis, MN, 1993), p. 136.

7 Ibid., p. 137.

8 Vincent Descombes, *Modern French Philosophy*, trans. L. Scott-Fox and J. M. Harding (Cambridge, 1980), p. 61.

9 Lyotard, *Phenomenology*, p. 133, n. 1.

10 Ibid., p. 32.

11 Gayle Ormiston, 'Foreword' in Lyotard, *Phenomenology*, p. 2.

12 Lyotard, *Phenomenology*, p. 33.

13 Ibid., pp. 112–13.

14 Ibid., p. 122.

15 Ibid., p. 127.

16 Ibid., p. 128.

17 Ibid., p. 129.

18 Jean-François Lyotard, *Peregrinations: Law, Form, Event* (New York, 1988), p. 65.

19 Cornelius Castoriadis, 'Presentation of Socialisme ou Barbarie' (1949), in David Curtis, ed. *The Castoriadis Reader* (Oxford, 1997), p. 37.

20 For Castoriadis' overview of S. ou B., see Castoriadis, *The Castoriadis Reader*. The dominant French text is Philippe Gottraux, *'Socialisme ou Barbarie': un engagement politique et intellectuel dans la France de l'après-guerre* (Lausanne, 1997), and the only publication in English is Stephen Hastings-King, *Looking for the Proletariat*, which gives prominence to the account of Mothé.

21 Castoriadis, *The Castoriadis Reader*, p. xvi.

22 Daniel Mothé, 1955. Quoted in Amparo Vega, *Le Premier Lyotard: Philosophie critique et politique* (Paris, 2010), p. 100.

23 Jean-François Lyotard and Pierre Vidal-Naquet, 'Lyotard et Vidal-Naquet: Parler encore de la guerre d'Algérie', *Libération* (9 November 1989), pp. 31–2.

24 Marie-Pierre Ulloa, *Francis Jeanson: Un intellectuel en dissidence de la résistance à la guerre d'Algérie* (Paris, 2001). See pp. 181–8: 'La divergence idéologique Jeanson/Curiel'.

25 Frédéric Thomas, 'Inédit: Entretien avec quelques anciens membres de Socialisme ou Barbarie', *dissidences blog* (2014), www.dissidences. hypotheses.org, accessed 10 December 2015.

4 1968

1 Jean-Michel Salanskis, 'Préface: Le philosophe de la dépossession', *Lyotard à Nanterre*, ed. Claire Pagès (Paris, 2010).

2 Jean-François Lyotard, *Discourse, Figure*, trans. Antony Hudek and Mary Lydon (Minneapolis, MN, 2011), p. 14.

3 Michel Butor, 'Excuse en orbite', *Lyotard* [reprint of *L'Arc* 64 (1976)], ed. C. Clément and G. Lascault (Paris, 2010), p. 213.

4 Michel Butor, 'Recollections on Jean-François Lyotard', *Yale French Studies*, 99 (2001), pp. 7–8.

5 Ibid., p. 8.

6 Jean-François Lyotard, *Political Writings*, trans. Bill Readings and Kevin Paul Geiman (Minneapolis, MN, 1993), p. 255. Original emphasis.

7 Philippe Gottraux, *'Socialisme ou Barbarie': un engagement politique et intellectuel dans la France de l'après-guerre* (Lausanne, 1997), p. 106.

8 Sébastien de Diesbach, *La Révolution impossible: mes années avec Socialisme ou Barbarie* (Paris, 2013), p. 167.

9 Corinne Enaudeau, 'Introduction', in Jean-François Lyotard, *Why Philosophize?*, trans. Andrew Brown (London, 2013), p. 3.

10 Lyotard, *Why Philosophize?*, pp. 113, 115.

11 Ibid., p. 117.

12 See the posthumous collection: Jean-François Lyotard, *Logique de Levinas*, ed. Paul Audi (Paris, 2015).

13 Henri Lefebvre, 'Enquêtes sur les causes des manifestations' (11 May 1968),

in Lukasz Stanek, *Henri Lefebvre on Space: Architecture, Urban Research and the Production of Space* (Minneapolis, MN, 2011), p. 186.

14 Lyotard, *Political Writings*, p. 35.

15 Fonds Lyotard, Bibliothèque Doucet: JFL 490.

16 Pierre Vidal-Naquet, *Mémoires: 2. Le trouble et la lumière (1955–1998)* (Paris, 1998), p. 291. Lyotard makes reference to the pamphlet 'Votre lutte est la nôtre' in *Pérégrinations* (Paris, 1990), p. 113.

17 Daniel and Gabriel Cohn-Bendit, *Obsolete Communism: The Left-wing Alternative* (London, 1968), p. 18; Henri Lefebvre and Kirsten Ross, 'Lefebvre and the Situationists: An Interview', *October*, 79 (1997), p. 6.

18 Hervé Bourges, ed., *The French Student Revolt: The Leaders Speak* (London, 1968), p. 58.

19 Lyotard, *Why Philosophize?*, p. 115.

20 Lyotard, *Political Writings*, p. 33.

21 Lyotard, *Discourse, Figure*, p. 7.

22 Bill Readings, *Introducing Lyotard: Art and Politics* (London and New York, 1991), p. xxv.

23 Kiff Bamford, 'Better Lyo*tard* than never, I figure', *Art History*, XXXVI/4 (2013), p. 885. Internal quotation: Lyotard, *Discourse, Figure*, p. 4.

24 Marx, cited in Lyotard, *Discourse, Figure*, p. 133.

25 Lyotard, *Discourse, Figure*, p. 135.

26 Ibid., p. 134.

27 Jean-Michel Salanskis, 'Difficile politique', *Cités*, 45 (2011), p. 19.

28 Jean-François Lyotard, *Dérive à partir de Marx et Freud* (Paris, 1973), p. 11.

5 *Dérive*

1 Jean-François Lyotard, *Driftworks*, ed. and trans. Roger McKeon (New York, 1984), p. 15.

2 Ibid., p. 16.

3 Ibid., p. 24.

4 Jean-François Lyotard, *Political Writings*, trans. Bill Readings and Kevin Paul Geiman (Minneapolis, MN, 1993), p. 67.

5 Bernard Lamarche-Vadel, *L'Abandon de la critique d'art* [video] (4 April 1989), La Villa Arson, Nice, www.villa-arson.org, accessed 15 December 2015.

6 Jean-François Lyotard, *Pacific Wall*, trans. Bruce Boone (Venice, CA, 1990), p. 9.

7 Jean-François Lyotard, *Postmodern Fables*, trans. Georges Van Den Abbeele (Minneapolis, MN, 1997), pp. 4, 14–15.

8 Interview with Corinne Enaudeau and Laurence Kahn, 25 September 2015.

9 Élisabeth Roudinesco, *Jacques Lacan and Co: A History of Psychoanalysis, 1925–1985*, trans. Jeffrey Mehlman (London, 1990), p. 377.

10 Jean-François Lyotard, *Discourse, Figure*, trans. Antony Hudek and Mary Lydon (Minneapolis, MN, 2011), p. 249.

11 Bill Readings, *Introducing Lyotard: Art and Politics* (London, 1991), p. 47. A useful résumé of this section of *Discourse, Figure* is given here: pp. 44–52.

12 Lyotard, *Discourse, Figure*, pp. 246, 9.

13 Ibid., p. 233.

14 Personal communication with Roger McKeon.

15 Quoted in Sarah Wilson, 'Epilogue', Jean-François Lyotard, *The Assassination of Experience by Painting, Monory* (Leuven, 2013), p. 250.

16 Fluxus: a loose international network of artists, poets and composers who challenged conventions of display, dissemination and participation, particularly in the 1960s and 1970s.

17 Jean-François Lyotard, *Discours, figure* (Paris, 1971), p. 11; Jean-François Lyotard, *Libidinal Economy*, trans. Iain Hamilton Grant (London, 2004), p. 256.

18 Lyotard, *Libidinal Economy*, pp. 1–2.

19 Ibid., p. 3.

20 Ibid., pp. 133, 135.

21 Jean-François Lyotard and Jean-Loup Thébaud, *Just Gaming*, trans. Wlad Godzich (Minneapolis, MN, 1985), p. 3.

22 Friedrich Nietzsche, *The Gay Science*, trans. Josefine Nauckhoff (Cambridge, 2001), §366.

23 U.E.C. Nanterre, *Connaissance de l'idéologie*, vol. 1 (Paris, 1969), with thanks to Roger McKeon for access to this pamphlet and highlighting the quoted remark.

24 Gilles Deleuze, 'Appréciation' of J-F Lyotard's *Discours, figure*', *La Quinzaine littéraire*, 140 (1 May 1972), p. 19.

25 Quoted in François Dosse, *Gilles Deleuze and Félix Guattari: Intersecting Lives*, trans. Deborah Glassman (New York, 2011), p. 353.

26 Jean-François Lyotard, 'Notes on the Return and Kapital', trans. Roger McKeon, *Semiotext(e)*, III /I (1977), p. 47.

27 Ibid.

6 'A Report on Knowledge'

1 Jean-François Lyotard, *The Differend: Phrases in Dispute*, trans. Georges Van Den Abbeele (Manchester, 1988), p. xiv.

2 Alain Badiou, 'Custos, quid noctis?', *Critique*, 450 (November 1984), p. 851.

3 Geoffrey Bennington, *Lyotard: Writing the Event* (Manchester, 1988), p. 2.

4 Stuart Sim, *Jean-François Lyotard* (Hemel Hempstead, 1996), p. 30.

5 Jean-François Lyotard, *The Postmodern Condition: A Report on Knowledge*, trans. Geoff Bennington and Brian Massumi (Manchester, 1984), p. xxiv.

6 Ibid.

7 Ibid., p. 45.

8 Jean-François Lyotard, *Les Transformateurs Duchamp/Duchamp's TRANS/formers*, trans. Ian McLeod (Leuven, 2010), pp. 76–7.

9 Gilles Aillaud, Eduardo Arroyo and Antonio Recalcati, *Vivre et laisser mourir, ou la fin tragique de Marcel Duchamp* (Live and Let Die, or the Tragic End of Marcel Duchamp), oil on canvas, polyptych (eight pieces), 163 x 992 cm, 1965, Museo Reina Sofia Madrid.

10 Lyotard, *Duchamp*, pp. 51, 193; Amelia Jones, *Postmodernism and the En-gendering of Marcel Duchamp* (Cambridge, 1994), p. 101.

11 Lynda Nead, *The Female Nude: Art, Obscenity and Sexuality* (London, 1992), p. 11.

12 Lyotard, *Duchamp*, pp. 184–5.

13 Ibid., p. 49.

14 Ibid.

15 Ibid.

16 Jean-François Lyotard, *Karel Appel: Un geste de couleur/Karel Appel: A Gesture of Colour*, trans. Vlad Ionescu and Peter Milne (Leuven, 2009) pp. 38–9, translation modified.

17 Lyotard, *The Postmodern Condition*, p. xxv.

18 Jean-François Lyotard, *Les Problèmes du savoir dans les sociétés industrielles les plus développés* (Quebec City, 1979), p. 2.

19 Lyotard, *The Postmodern Condition*, p. xxv, translation modified.

20 David Macey, *The Lives of Michel Foucault* (New York, 1993), p. 222.

21 Ibid., p. 225.

22 Ibid., p. 228.

23 Alain Badiou, *Deleuze: The Clamour of Being*, trans. Louise Burchill (Minneapolis, MN, 2000), p. 1.

24 Alain Badiou, *Pocket Pantheon*, trans. David Macey (London and New York, 2009), p. 108.

25 Nicolas Rousseau, 'Entretien avec Pascal Auger', *Actu Philosophia* (11 July 2011), www.actu-philosophia.com, accessed 15 March 2016.

26 Fonds Lyotard, Bibliothèque littéraire Jacques Doucet, JFL 10–1, mimeographed double-sided sheet on pink paper included in archive records of Lyotard's seminar course at Vincennes (1 November 1971).

27 Personal communication with Pierre Merlin, whose wife, Madeleine Jullien – head of the library at Vincennes from 1979 – followed Lyotard's course with enthusiasm.

28 Christian Descamps and Jean-François Lyotard, 'Entretien', *La Quinzaine littéraire*, 322 (1980), p. 20.

29 Rousseau, 'Entretien'.

30 Dominique Grisoni, ed., *Politiques de la philosophie: Châtelet, Derrida, Foucault, Lyotard, Serres* (Paris, 1976), p. 11.

31 Hugh J. Silverman, ed., *Lyotard: Philosophy, Politics, and the Sublime* (New York, 2002), p. 16.

32 Danto cited in Sylvère Lotringer and Sande Cohen, *French Theory in America* (New York, 2001), p. 2.

33 Ibid.

34 Sylvère Lotringer and David Morris, eds, *Schizo-Culture: The Event* (Cambridge, MA, 2014), p. 21.

35 Jean-François Lyotard, *Toward the Postmodern*, ed. Robert Harvey and Mark S. Roberts (Atlantic Highlands, NJ, 1993), p. 64.

36 Ibid., p. 68.

37 Jean-François Lyotard, *Political Writings*, trans. Bill Readings and Kevin Paul Geiman (Minneapolis, MN, 1993), pp. 70, 74.

38 'Département et Institut Polytechnique de Philosophie Année 1981–2', Library of the University of Paris 8, digital archives (1982), www.bibliotheque-numerique-paris8.fr, accessed 8 March 2016.

39 Lyotard, *The Postmodern Condition*, pp. 44, 47.

7 Les Immatériaux

1 Jean-François Lyotard, 'Qui a peur des "Immatériaux"?', *Le Monde* (3 May 1985), quoted in John Rajchman, 'The Postmodern Museum', *Art in America* (October 1985), p. 114; Centre Georges Pompidou, *Immaterials: English Version of the French Sound Track* (Paris, 1985), p. 14.

2 Hans Ulrich Obrist, 'After the Moderns, The Immaterials', *The Exhibitionist*, 5 (January 2012), p. 12.

3 Bernard Blistène, 'A Conversation with Jean-François Lyotard', *Flash Art*, 122 (March 1985), p. 33.

4 Chantal Noël, ed., *Les Immatériaux: album* (Paris, 1985), p.5. Blistène, 'A Conversation', p. 34.

5 Yuk Hui and Andreas Broeckmann, eds, *30 Years after Les Immatériaux: Art, Science, and Theory* (Lüneburg, 2015); *Les Immatériaux, trente ans après*, conference, 27 November 2015, Centre Georges Pompidou, Paris.

6 Nathalie Heinich, 'Les Immatériaux Revisited: Innovation in Innovations', *Tate Papers*, 12 (autumn 2009), Tate, www.tate.org.uk, accessed 26 February 2014; Jérôme Glicenstein, 'Les Immatériaux: exposition, oeuvre, événement', in *Lyotard et les arts*, ed. F. Coblence and M. Enaudeau (Paris, 2014).

7 Jean-François Lyotard, 'Les Immatériaux' (1984), trans. Paul Smith, in *Thinking about Exhibitions*, ed. Reesa Greenberg et al. (London, 1996), p. 159.

8 Heinich, 'Les Immatériaux Revisited', §9.

9 Samuel Beckett, 'Fizzles 4', in Pompidou, *Immaterials: English Version*, p. 3.

10 Lyotard, 'Les Immatériaux' (1984), p. 161.

11 Ibid., p. 165.

12 Antony Hudek, 'From Over- to Sub-exposure: The Anamnesis of *Les Immatériaux*', in Hui and Broeckmann, ed., *30 Years after*, p. 72.

13 Élie Théofilakis, ed., *Modernes, et après? "Les Immatériaux"* (Paris, 1985), p. 15.

14 Centre Georges Pompidou, *Les Immatériaux: Dossier de presse* (Paris, 1985), Archives du Centre Georges Pompidou, www.centrepompidou. fr, accessed 27 February 2016.

15 Blistène, 'A Conversation with Jean-François Lyotard', p. 32.

16 Rolf Gehlhaar, 'Sound=Space in *Les Immatériaux* at the Centre Pompidou, Paris' (*c*. 1986), www.gehlhaar.org, accessed 3 March 2016.

17 Interview with Dolorès Lyotard, 26 November 2015; 'Jean-Louis Boissier in conversation with Andreas Broeckmann: The Production of *Les Immatériaux*', in Hui and Broeckmann, ed., *30 Years After*, p. 99.

18 Christian Delacampagne, 'Une Philosophie post-moderne', *Le Monde* (24 February 1984), www.lemonde.fr, accessed 10 January 2016.

19 Fonds Lyotard, Bibliothèque littéraire Jacques Doucet: JFL 541; 'Introduction à une étude du politique selon Kant', in Jean-Luc Nancy and Philippe Lacoue-Labarthe, eds, *Rejouer le politique* (Paris, 1981), pp. 91–134.

20 Jean-François Lyotard, *The Lyotard Reader*, ed. Andrew Benjamin (Oxford, 1989), p. 127.

21 Jean-François Lyotard and Thierry Chaput, *Épreuves d'écriture* (Paris, 1985), p. 6.

22 Mireille Calle, 'Entretien avec Jean-François Lyotard', *Les Métamorphoses Butor* (Sainte-Foy, Québec, 1991), p. 71 ; Benoît Peeters, *Derrida: A Biography*, trans. Andrew Brown (Cambridge, 2013), p. 376.

23 Jacques Derrida, 'Writing-proofs' and Jean-François Lyotard 'Translator's Notes', trans. Roland-François Lack, *Pli: The Warwick Journal of Philosophy*, 6 (1997), pp. 37–57.

24 Cited in Hudek, 'From Over- to Sub-exposure', pp. 76–7.

25 Jean-François Lyotard, *The Postmodern Condition: A Report on Knowledge*, trans. Geoff Bennington and Brian Massumi (Manchester, 1984), p. 10.

26 Jean-François Lyotard, *The Differend: Phrases in Dispute*, trans. Georges Van Den Abbeele (Manchester, 1988), p. xii.

27 Lyotard, 'Les Immatériaux' (1984), p. 169.

28 Heinich, 'Les Immatériaux Revisited', up §13.

29 Antony Hudek, 'The Affective Economy of the Lyotardian Archive', in *Rereading Jean-François Lyotard: Essays on his Later Works*, ed., Heidi Bickis and Rob Shields (Farnham, 2013), p. 19.

30 Lyotard in Blistène, 'A Conversation with Jean-François Lyotard', p. 35.

8 'A Blind Spot'

1 Jean-François Lyotard, *Driftworks*, ed. and trans. Roger McKeon (New York, 1984), p. 19, translation modified.

2 Max Gallo, 'Les Intellectuels, la politique et la modernité', *Le Monde* (26 July 1983), p. 7.

3 Jean-François Lyotard, 'Tombeau de l'intellectuel', *Le Monde* (8 October 1983), pp. 1–2; trans. in Lyotard, *Political Writings*, trans. Bill Readings and Kevin Paul Geiman (Minneapolis, MN, 1993), pp. 3–7.

4 Lyotard, *Political Writings*, p. 6.

5 Jean-François Lyotard, 'Foreword: A Success of Sartre's', trans. Jeffrey Mehlman, in Denis Hollier, *The Politics of Prose* (Minneapolis, MN, 1986), p. xi.

6 Interview with Patricia Azevedo, 15 December 2015.

7 Jean-François Lyotard, *Lessons on the Analytic of the Sublime*, trans. Elizabeth Rottenberg (Stanford, CA, 1994), pp. ix–x.

8 Ibid., p. 7.

9 Christine Buci-Glucksmann, 'À propos du *Différend*: Entretien avec J.-F. Lyotard', *Les Cahiers de Philosophie*, 5 (Spring 1988), p. 44.

10 David Carroll, 'Memorial for the Différend: In Memory of J.-F. Lyotard', *Parallax*, VI/4 (2000), p 6.

11 Quoted in Avital Ronell, 'The Differends of Man', *Diacritics*, 19 (1988), p. 70.

12 Manfred Frank, *The Boundaries of Agreement* (Aurora, CO, 2005).

13 Lyotard, *Political Writings*, p. 137.

14 Ibid., p. 140.

15 Jean-François Lyotard, *Heidegger and 'the jews'*, trans. Andreas Michel and Mark Roberts (Minneapolis, MN, 1990), p. 52.

16 Jacques Derrida, 'Préjugés: Devant la loi', in *La Faculté de juger: Colloque de Cerisy* (Paris, 1985), p. 98.

17 Jacques Derrida, 'The Ends of Man', trans. Alan Bass, in *Margins of Philosophy* (Chicago, IL, 1984), p. 136.

18 Benoît Peeters, *Derrida: A Biography*, trans. Andrew Brown (Cambridge, 2013), p. 242.

19 Ibid., p. 246.

20 Interview with Dalia Judovitz, 13 May 2016.

21 Jean-François Lyotard, 'On the Strength of the Weak', trans. Roger McKeon, *Semiotext(e)*, III/2 (1978), p. 206.

22 Gilles Deleuze, 'Lettre à Jean-François Lyotard', *Europe: Revue littéraire mensuelle* (May 2008), p. 264.

23 Interviews with Corinne Enaudeau, 25 September 2015, and Dolorès Lyotard, 26 November 2015. The question was prompted by Lyotard's assertion that Deleuze was 'one of the two geniuses of our philosophical generation', reprinted in Jean-François Lyotard, *Misère de la philosophie*, ed. Dolorès Lyotard (Paris, 2000), p. 194.

24 Ronell, 'The Differends of Man', p. 66.

25 Jean-François Lyotard, *The Lyotard Reader*, ed. Andrew Benjamin (Oxford, 1989), p. 368.

26 Ibid., p. 388, translation modified.

27 Ibid., p. 368.

28 Michèle Cohen-Halimi, *Stridence spéculative: Adorno, Lyotard, Derrida* (Paris, 2014), p. 32. Thanks to Étienne Balibar for drawing my attention to this publication.

29 Ibid., p. 34.

30 Lyotard, *The Lyotard Reader*, p. 388.

31 Jacques Derrida, 'Lyotard and "Us"', in *Minima Memoria: Essays in the Wake of Jean-François Lyotard*, ed. Claire Nouvet et al. (Stanford, CA, 2007), pp. 1–26.

32 Lyotard, *The Lyotard Reader*, p. 388.

33 Jean-François Lyotard, *Discourse, Figure*, trans. Antony Hudek and Mary Lydon (Minneapolis, MN, 2011), p. 115; cited in Derrida, 'Préjugés: Devant la loi', p. 92.

34 For a discussion of Lyotard's use of the sublime and its reception, see Chapter Four 'The Sublime', in Kiff Bamford, *Lyotard and the 'figural' in Performance, Art and Writing* (London, 2012).

35 Willem van Reijen and Dick Veerman, 'An Interview with Jean-François Lyotard' [1987], *Theory, Culture and Society*, V/2 (1988), p. 284.

36 Jean-François Lyotard, *The Inhuman: Reflections on Time*, trans. Geoffrey Bennington and Rachel Bowlby (London, 1988), pp. 119–28.

37 Ibid., p. 125.

38 Ibid.

39 David Carroll, *Paraesthetics: Foucault, Lyotard, Derrida* (New York and London, 1987), p. XIV.

40 Lyotard, *Heidegger*, p. 47.

9 Childhood without Conclusion

1 Jean-François Lyotard, 'Infans', trans. Mary Lydon in Mary Lydon, 'Veduta on *Discours, figure*', *Yale French Studies*, 99 (2001), p. 25.

2 Lydon, 'Veduta', p. 10. Mary Lydon published translations of two chapters of *Discours, figure* before her early death in 2001; these are incorporated into the translation of 2011 by Lydon and Antony Hudek.

3 Lydon 'Veduta', p. 17.

4 Dolorès Lyotard, 'Presentation to 'À l'écrit bâté' – Lettre perpétuelle', trans. Rob Shields, in *Rereading Jean-François Lyotard: Essays on his Later Works*, ed. Heidi Bickis and Rob Shields (Farnham, 2013), p. 69; interview with Dolorès Lyotard, 26 November 2015.

5 Dolorès Lyotard, 'Presentation to 'À l'écrit bâté', pp. 69–70.

6 Jean-François Lyotard, *Misère de la philosophie*, ed. Dolorès Lyotard (Paris, 2000), pp. 153–74; Jean-François Lyotard, 'To Burdened Writing', trans. Stephen Barker, in *Rereading Jean-François Lyotard*, ed. Bickis and Shields, pp. 74–80.

7 Jean-François Lyotard, 'Retour', *Lectures d'enfance* (Paris, 1991), p. 11.

8 Jean-François Lyotard, *The Inhuman: Reflections on Time*, trans. Geoffrey Bennington and Rachel Bowlby (London, 1988), p. 2.

9 Jean-François Lyotard, *Que Peindre? Adami, Arakawa, Buren/What to Paint? Adami, Arakawa, Buren*, trans. Antony Hudek (Leuven, 2012), p. 239. See Jean-François Lyotard, *Textes dispersés II/Miscellaneous Texts II*, ed. Hermann Parret (Leuven, 2012), pp. 562–3.

10 Jean-François Lyotard, *Signed, Malraux*, trans. Robert Harvey (Minneapolis, MN, 1999), p. 302.

11 Dolorès Lyotard, 'Forewarning', in Jean-François Lyotard, *The Confession of Augustine*, trans. Richard Beardsworth (Stanford, CA, 2000), p. ix.

12 Francis Guibal and Jacob Rogozinski, *Témoigner du différend: Quand phraser ne se peut* (Paris, 1989), p. 61.

13 Jean-François Lyotard, 'Emma', in *Lyotard: Philosophy, Politics, and the Sublime*, ed. Hugh J. Silverman (New York, 2002), pp. 29, 30.

14 Lyotard, *The Inhuman*, p. 54.

15 Ibid., p. 77.

16 Philippe Lançon, 'Jean-François Lyotard, 72 ans, moine-militant devenu philosophe a publié un (beau) livre sur Malraux', *Libération* (23 November 1996), www.liberation.fr, accessed 16 October 2015.

17　Jean-François Lyotard, 'Foreword', in Philippe Bonnefis, *Céline: The Recall of the Birds*, trans. Paul Weidmann (Minneapolis, MN, 1996), pp. ix, xix.

18　Jean-François Lyotard, *Signé Malraux* (Paris, 1996), back cover.

19　Website of the Robert W. Woodruff foundation. See www.woodruff. org, accessed 30 April 2016.

20　Malraux cited in Lyotard, *Signed*, p. 210. See Dolorès Lyotard, 'L'Hypothèse autographique de Jean-François Lyotard', in *Signés Malraux: André Malraux et la question biographique*, ed. Martine Boymer-Weinmann and Jean-Louis Jeannelle (Paris, 2016), pp. 185–206.

21　Lyotard, *Signed*, p. 210.

22　Interview with Dolorès Lyotard, 26 November 2015; see Dolorès Lyotard, 'L'Hypothèse autographique', pp. 185–206.

23　Lyotard, *The Inhuman*, p. 20.

24　Lyotard, *Signed*, p. 263.

25　Ibid., p. 264.

26　Jean-Louis Jeannelle, 'Outre-tombe des mémories', in *Signés Malraux: André Malraux et la question biographique*, ed. Martine Boymer-Weinmann and Jean-Louis Jeannelle (Paris, 2016), p. 207.

27　Lyotard, *Signed*, p. 196.

28　Ibid., p. 2.

29　Fonds Lyotard, Bibliothèque littéraire Jacques Doucet: JFL 538.

30　Lançon, 'Jean-François Lyotard'.

31　Lyotard, *The Confession*, p. 26.

32　Jean-François Lyotard, *Soundproof Room: Malraux's Anti-aesthetics*, trans. Robert Harvey (Stanford, CA, 2001), p. 2.

33　Ibid., p. 7.

34　Lyotard, *Que Peindre?*, p. 109.

35　Jean-François Lyotard, *Heidegger and 'the jews'*, trans. Andreas Michel and Mark Roberts (Minneapolis, MN, 1990), p. 40.

Select Bibliography

Lyotard in English Translation

The Assassination of Experience by Painting, Monory, trans. Rachel Bowlby (Leuven, 2013)

The Confession of Augustine, trans. Richard Beardsworth (Stanford, CA, 2000)

The Differend: Phrases in Dispute, trans. Georges Van Den Abbeele (Manchester, 1988)

Discourse, Figure, trans. Antony Hudek and Mary Lydon (Minneapolis, MN, 2011)

Driftworks, ed. and trans. Roger McKeon (New York, 1984)

Heidegger and 'the jews', trans. Andreas Michel and Mark Roberts (Minneapolis, MN, 1990)

The Hyphen: Between Judaism and Christianity, with Eberhard Gruber, trans. Pascale-Anne Brault and Michael Naas (Amherst, NY, 1999)

The Inhuman: Reflections on Time, trans. Geoffrey Bennington and Rachel Bowlby (London, 1988)

Just Gaming, with Jean-Loup Thébaud, trans. Wlad Godzich (Minneapolis, MN, 1985)

Karel Appel: Un Geste de couleur/Karel Appel: A Gesture of Colour, trans. Vlad Ionescu and Peter Milne (Leuven, 2009)

Lessons on the Analytic of the Sublime, trans. Elizabeth Rottenberg (Stanford, CA, 1994)

Libidinal Economy, trans. Iain Hamilton Grant (London, 1993)

The Lyotard Reader, ed. Andrew Benjamin (Oxford, 1989)

Lyotard Reader and Guide, ed. Keith Crome and James Williams (Edinburgh, 2006)

Pacific Wall, trans. Bruce Boone (Venice, CA, 1990)

Peregrinations: Law, Form, Event (New York, 1988)

Phenomenology, trans. Brian Beakley (New York, 1991)

Political Writings, trans. Bill Readings and Kevin Paul Geiman
  (Minneapolis, MN, 1993)

The Postmodern Condition: A Report on Knowledge, trans. Geoff Bennington
  and Brian Massumi (Manchester, 1984)

The Postmodern Explained to Children: Correspondence 1982–1985,
  trans. Julian Pefanis, Morgan Thomas, et al. (London, 1992)

*Que Peindre? Adami, Arakawa, Buren/What to Paint? Adami, Arakawa,
  Buren*, trans. Antony Hudek (Leuven, 2012)

Signed, Malraux, trans. Robert Harvey (Minneapolis, MN, 1999)

Soundproof Room: Malraux's Anti-aesthetics, trans. Robert Harvey
  (Stanford, CA, 2001)

Toward the Postmodern, ed. Robert Harvey and Mark S. Roberts
  (Atlantic Highlands, NJ, 1993)

Les Transformateurs Duchamp/Duchamp's TRANS/formers, trans. Ian
  McLeod (Leuven, 2010)

Why Philosophize?, trans. Andrew Brown (London, 2013)

Selected Works on Lyotard

Bamford, Kiff, *Lyotard and the 'figural' in Performance, Art and Writing*
  (London, 2012)

Bennington, Geoffrey, *Lyotard: Writing the Event* (Manchester, 1988)

Bickis, Heidi and Rob Shields, eds, *Rereading Jean-François Lyotard: Essays
  on his Later Works* (Farnham, 2013)

Coblence, Françoise, and Michel Enaudeau, eds, *Lyotard et les arts*
  (Paris, 2014)

Costa, Antonio and Raoul Kirchmayr, eds, 'L'acinema di Lyotard', *Aut Aut*,
  338 (Milan, 2008)

Durafour, Jean-Michel, *Jean-François Lyotard: Questions au cinéma*
  (Paris, 2009)

Enaudeau, Corinne, et al., eds, *Les Transformateurs Lyotard* (Paris, 2008)

De Fontnay, Elisabeth, *Une tout autre histoire: Questions à Jean-François
  Lyotard* (Paris, 2006)

Gaillard, Julie, et al., eds, *Traversals of Affect: On Jean-François Lyotard*
  (London, 2016)

Gallo, Francesca, *Les Immatériaux: Un percorso di Jean-François Lyotard nell'arte contemporanea* (Rome, 2008).

Harvey, Robert and Lawrence R. Scher, eds, 'Jean-François Lyotard: Time and Judgement', *Yale French Studies*, 99 (2001)

Jones, Graham, *Lyotard Reframed* (London, 2014)

Malpas, Simon, *Jean-François Lyotard* (London, 2002)

Nouvet, Claire, Zrinka Stahuljak and Kent Still, eds, *Minima Memoria: Essays in the Wake of Jean-François Lyotard* (Stanford, CA, 2007)

Pagès, Claire, *Lyotard et l'aliénation* (Paris, 2011)

Readings, Bill, *Introducing Lyotard: Art and Politics* (London and New York, 1991)

Robbins, Derek, ed., *Jean-François Lyotard*, 3 vols (London, 2004)

Sfez, Gérald, *Lyotard: La faculté d'une phrase* (Paris, 2000)

Silverman, Hugh J., ed., *Lyotard: Philosophy, Politics, and the Sublime* (New York, 2002)

Taylor, Victor E., and Gregg Lambert, eds, *Jean-François Lyotard: Critical Evaluations in Cultural Theory*, 3 vols (London, 2006)

Williams, James, *Lyotard: Toward a Postmodern Philosophy* (London, 1998)

—, *Lyotard and the Political* (London, 2000)

Woodward, Ashley, and Graham Jones, eds, *Acinemas: Lyotard's Philosophy of Film* (Edinburgh, 2017)

Wunderlich, Antonia, *Der Philosoph in Museum: Die Ausstetlung 'Les Immatériaux' von Jean-François Lyotard* (Bielefeld, 2008)

Zarka, Yves Charles, ed., 'Lyotard politique', *Cités*, 45 (2011)

Context

Badiou, Alain, *Pocket Pantheon*, trans. David Macey (London and New York, 2009)

Castoriadis, Cornelius, *The Castoriadis Reader*, ed. David Curtis (Oxford, 1997)

Cohen-Halimi, Michèle, *Stridence spéculative: Adorno, Lyotard, Derrida* (Paris, 2014)

Cusset, François, *How Foucault, Derrida, Deleuze, and Co. Transformed the Intellectual Life of the United States*, trans. Jeff Fort (Minneapolis, MN, 2008)

Descombes, Vincent, *Modern French Philosophy*, trans. L. Scott-Fox and
    J. M. Harding (Cambridge, 1980)
Dosse, François, *Gilles Deleuze and Félix Guattari: Intersecting Lives*, trans.
    Deborah Glassman (New York, 2011)
Gildea, Robert, *France Since 1945* (Oxford, 2002)
Gottraux, Philippe, *'Socialisme ou Barbarie': Un engagement politique et
    intellectuel dans la France de l'après-guerre* (Lausanne, 1997)
Hastings-King, Stephen, *Looking for the Proletariat: Socialisme ou Barbarie
    and the Problem of Worker Writing* (Chicago, IL, 2015)
Hui, Yuk, and Andreas Broeckmann, eds, *30 Years after Les Immatériaux:
    Art, Science, and Theory* (Lüneburg, 2015)
Lotringer, Sylvère, and Sande Cohen, *French Theory in America*
    (New York, 2001)
Lyotard, Jean-François, Jacques Derrida, et al., *La Faculté de juger*
    (Paris, 1985)
Macey, David, *The Lives of Michel Foucault* (New York, 1993)
Peeters, Benoît, *Derrida: A Biography*, trans. Andrew Brown
    (Cambridge, 2013)
Roudinesco, Élisabeth, *Jacques Lacan and Co: A History of Psychoanalysis
    1925–1985*, trans. Jeffrey Mehlman (London, 1990)
Sarah Wilson, *The Visual World of French Theory: Figurations* (New Haven,
    CT, and London, 2010)
Schrift, Alan D., *Twentieth-century French Philosophy* (London, 2006)
Vidal-Naquet, Pierre, *Mémoires: 2. Le trouble et la lumière (1955–1998)*
    (Paris, 1998)

Acknowledgements

I am most grateful to have had the opportunity to speak to members of Lyotard's family: his daughters Corinne Enaudeau and Laurence Kahn, and his second wife Dolorès Lyotard – and also for the use of photographs, several of which are included in this book. Thanks also to those who responded to my enquiries – Pascal Auger, Patricia Azevedo, Étienne Balibar, Andreas Broekmann, Jean Cohen, Andrew Feenberg, John Fekete, Dick Howard, Fredric Jameson, Dick Howard, John Johnston, Dalia Judovitz, Sylvère Lotringer, Roger McKeon, Pierre Merlin, Aurélian Moreau, Michel Spanin and James Williams – to the organizers of the conferences – *Lyotard et le langage* (Paris, 2015) and *Les Immatériaux, trente ans après* (Paris, 2015) – and to staff at the Bibliothèque littéraire Jacques Doucet and Bibliothèque Kandinsky. Andy Stafford and Roger McKeon kindly read the whole manuscript and Laurence Kahn checked the early sections.

Language difficulties were made much easier through the assistance of Marion Bouville, for the French, and J. M. and G. B. Bamford for the English. Thanks to Leeds Beckett University for research leave and to the School of Art, Architecture and Design for funding illustration costs. Lastly, thanks to all those who have had to listen: colleagues, friends and family – in particular, the long-suffering Izzy, Joseph and Jill.

Photo Acknowledgements

BASSIGNAC/GAILLARDE/MERILLON/ Gamma-Rapho via Getty Images: p. 150; Courtesy of Joanna Delorme © Editions Galilée, Paris: p. 92; Courtesy of Corinne Enaudeau: pp. 21, 26, 30, 43, 86; Getty/ Maurice Jarnoux: p. 13; Courtesy International Institute of Social History, Amsterdam, collection Paris, mouvement mai–juin 1968: p. 59; Courtesy of Dolorès Lyotard: pp. 6, 138, 145; Courtesy of Luc Maillet © Luc Maillet/ Grafibus: pp. 105, 107, 119; Courtesy of Andrew Feenberg, The May 1968 Events Archive, Simon Fraser University, Vancouver: p. 67; © Centre Pompidou, MNAM, Bibliothèque Kandinsky, photo by Jean-Claude Planchet: pp. 109, 111, 113, 117; Courtesy of Jack Shainman Gallery, New York © Michael Snow: pp. 82, 83; Courtesy of Pascal Auger and Michel Spanin, Photo by Michel Spanin: p. 99.